The Path to Job Search Success:

A Neuroscientific Approach to Interviewing, Negotiating and Networking

Tom Payne

The Path to Job Search Success:
A Neuroscientific Approach to Interviewing, Negotiating and Networking

Copyright © 2015 Tom Payne

ISBN-13: 978-1511489546
ISBN-10: 1511489545

All rights reserved. No part of this book may be used or reproduced by any means, graphic, electronic, or mechanical, including photocopying, recording, taping, or any information storage retrieval system without the written permission of the author except in the case of brief quotations embodied in critical articles and reviews.

CreateSpace Independent Publishing Platform

CONTENTS

PART 1: CHANGING COURSE

1. Amazing Results — 3
2. The Nature of the Game — 14
3. Who's Running the Show? — 22
4. Cognitive Ease, Cognitive Strain, and Clarity — 30

PART 2: MASTERING NON-VERBAL COMMUNICATION

5. The Power of Non-Verbal Behaviors — 43
6. Mastering Non-Verbal Communication — 54
7. Run for Your Life — 67
8. Survival of the Fit — 74

PART 3: MASTERING VERBAL COMMUNICATION

9. Self-Discovery — 85
10. The Branding Statement — 99
11. "Tell Me a Story" — 108
12. A Formula for Success — 114
13. The Making of a Story — 124
14. Become the Solution — 134
15. Scripted Answers — 142
16. Suicide Questions — 154

PART 4: FINISHING TOUCHES

17. The Interview's End Game — 171
18. Mock Interviews and Phone Interviews — 179
19. Networking Through Informational Interviews — 187
20. Technological Twists — 198
21. Negotiation — 207
22. The H.E.A.R.T. Principles — 219
    ACKNOWLEDGEMENTS — 235

PART 1:

CHANGING COURSE

1

Amazing Results

JACK'S NIGHTMARE SCENARIO

If accomplishments and giftedness determined job search success, then Jack should have had a job by now.[1] He scored a perfect 800 on the math section of the SAT, and had a post-graduate degree in engineering from Stanford University.

But, as Jack discovered, we are psychologically wired to move in the wrong direction down the job-search path. How we perceive things, make decisions, the many processes that make up human nature, can betray us. Fortunately, this is not an irreversible condition, and after weeks of hard work Jack was ready to take the next step.

I asked him to call a friend at the last place he worked to set up an informational interview. His goal was to learn about the current state of his former company, how their industry was faring, his possible fit within it, and to gather networking contacts.

They agreed to see him. Then, the day before his flight, he got a phone call and discovered…I'll let his emails tell the story:

---

[1] I am referring to all of my clients by a changed first name.

> Hi Tom,
>
> I wanted to drop you a quick note to let you know how my interviews went with my former company… and to thank you for all of your help.
>
> Last week I had interviews at both the Atlanta and Tampa offices. The initial plan was to just have general discussions about any potential future needs they might have. *The day before I was to arrive* [my emphasis] I got an agenda with a total of 18 separate interviews scheduled between the two offices. I was given a heads up before the interviews that there were some people that were against hiring me.

Yikes! He had less than twenty-four hours to prepare for eighteen job interviews in two days. And at least one of the interviewers, a former colleague who did not like Jack, wanted to block his return.

BRING IT ON

Most people would dread this scenario, but Jack did not. After the interviews he shared his results:

> It was a grueling couple of days but I ACED the interviews. Thanks in large part to your help the interviews couldn't have gone better. *Realizing the importance of style* and having some great *stories* that could be delivered *clearly* and *concisely* made the difference. [My emphasis.]

Now, even if you "ACED the interviews," what would you expect to hear at the end of them? Normally the hiring authority would say, "Thanks for your time," or, "We'll get back to you." After all, the eighteen people would need to discuss how he did, wouldn't they?

Jack heard something quite different. Again, I quote from his email:

> By the time I had completed the interviews I had won over even the people that were against hiring me and I was given the choice of either working in the Atlanta or Tampa office. I was told I will be receiving the official offer this Friday!

Instead of, "We'll get back to you," they asked him which office he wanted to work in. Can you imagine how he felt after conducting eighteen interviews and hearing this? And the news got better. When he received his offer he said he could not make a counteroffer on the salary, because their initial offer was at the top end of his position's pay scale. They had already maxed his salary out. That is a rare experience for most jobseekers, but it is not uncommon when you get the hiring authority to *want* you.

THE END RESULT

Jack's email concludes on a note that once again emphasizes the importance of style, or the way he presented himself:

> My biggest potential stumbling block was to explain my 6-year gap away from engineering. Going into the interview I felt confident that I could explain it in a way that turned it from a major negative into a non-event or even a positive. As a result of my preparation I was able to be relaxed, convey confidence and to be personable instead of being nervous and stiff.

The path that I took Jack down is deceptively simple. We aligned his job search actions with the way our minds and hearts work, how we process information, make decisions, are affected by hopes and fears, attitudes and assumptions, and so on. This realignment involved, in part, focusing on style.

THE CASE FOR STYLE

Realizing the importance of style was a turning point in Jack's quest for employment. Prior to this, he was misled by the false assumption that all he needed to do was to present his substantial, unadorned achievements, and he would be hired. He clung to this false assumption even while his experience proved it was wrong.

As I told Jack, "Credentials and qualifications get you an invitation to the contest, but they do not win it. Everyone who is being interviewed has substantial achievements, or they would not be there. Once the invitation to the interview is secured, it is how your achievements are presented that matter more than the achievements themselves."

To help Jack see the importance of style, I compared a very accomplished, style-challenged person with a less-accomplished, style-savvy competitor. The more accomplished person presented his bigger and better achievements as mere data-points, unadorned facts, a type of word cloud with a uniform font.

Meanwhile, his competitor presented her achievements in stories. They were like three-dimensional portraits competing against flat stick figures lacking depth. They also made her smaller achievements memorable, gave them context and did what a good story does: they entertained. By being entertaining she was more likable than some fact-centric, super-serious person.

I will compare a factual approach to stories so you can see, hear and feel the difference yourself.

COMPARING DATA-POINTS AND STORIES

In manufacturing there is a measurement of quality that looks at how many opportunities you had to make a mistake, and how many mistakes you made. If your quality level is 1,000 defects per million opportunities, then it is appalling. In this comparison, Jill improved her company's quality level from this abysmal level to ten defects per million opportunities, a 100-fold improvement.

Jill was competing for this job opportunity against Bob, a manufacturing genius, who improved a woeful quality rate of 1,000 defects per million opportunities to five defects per million opportunities. His achievement was twice as substantial as Jill's.

During their interviews, both were asked, "What achievement are you proudest of?"

Jill answered:

> When I joined Acme it had a reputation for putting out the lowest-quality product in our industry and for having the highest manufacturing costs.[2] Worse yet, the manufacturing

---

[2] Acme is my preferred name for a fictional company. You will encounter it, and variations of it, several times throughout this book.

team I was inheriting finished dead last in the company's job satisfaction surveys, and had high turnover.

To turn this situation around I developed a plan with measurable milestones, and whenever we achieved one we would have a mini-celebration. We worked together on process improvements that built quality into the product.

Before you knew it, we became a motivated team and we reduced the failure rate 100-fold. It went from 1,000 defects per million opportunities, to ten. This resulted in annual gains of $2,000,000 to the bottom line. I'm very proud of that, but what really warms my heart is the way our internal surveys showed my manufacturing team went from being the least satisfied employees in the company to among the most satisfied.

The interviewer looked at Jill and thought, "This woman is a transformational leader. Imagine what she could do for us. $2,000,000 to the bottom line!" And then it was Bob's turn to answer the same question.

THE FOG OF DATA

The interviewer asks Bob, "What achievement are you proudest of?"

Bob answers, "I'm proudest of the way I improved the quality of our manufacturing process. I reduced the error rate from 1,000 defects per million opportunities to five per million." A self-satisfied smile followed, along with silence. "Let that stunning achievement sink in," Bob thought, "then let's see if any of my competitors can top that." It was a great achievement. It made Bob feel good about himself whenever he thought about it.

"Wow," said the interviewer, "that's fantastic." But the interview doesn't end there. Bob's ineffective *style* is again illustrated by his answer to the interviewer's follow-up question, "How did you achieve this improvement in quality?"

This opened the door for Bob to lurch from one unpremeditated detail to the next. A flood of unnecessary words accompanied these details. His answer was like a rushed first draft in need of serious editing. Far from being like Jack's answers, "clear and concise," Bob's answer was stylistically awful. It is also punctuated by the "ummms" and "ahhhs" of someone who is trying to recall an answer:

> The steps I took to achieve this, I'm sure you can imagine, were many. Ummm.... There were dozens of Monday morning meetings to analyze data about every aspect of the manufacturing process. There was a constant reviewing of personnel. Two people were fired and two people were hired to replace them, and two people were promoted. My expectations were clearly spelled out in individual and group meetings and they were put in writing. Ahhh.... Some of the biggest gains came from improving the way we handled the work-in-process. I instituted completely new process controls, and changed some processes completely. I located processes that were causing a higher failure rate and removed them. That was big. Ummmm.... I bought some better error-tracking software and calibration devices. But as I look back, those Monday morning meetings turned out to be one of the most important game changers.

As the data tsunami gathered steam, and the meaningless facts multiplied, the truly great 200-fold improvement in quality was minimized, if not forgotten. It was buried in an unhappy fog of details. It was a proudly stated achievement framed by white noise, a background that deadened the sound of this great accomplishment.

There are reasons why data dumps occur. No one knows *his* achievements like the interviewee.[3] He loves the details surrounding his accomplishments, but because he hasn't edited them he ends up sharing too many, leaving the interviewer dazed. Suddenly, after experiencing a few data dumps, the hiring

---

[3] Until someone comes up with an acceptable gender-neutral pronoun, I suggest male writers use masculine pronouns and female writers use feminine pronouns.

authority doesn't want to hire this candidate for reasons he doesn't fully understand.

The key is this: Outstanding achievements can lose their impact when they are poorly presented. Style trumps substance, because a lack of style can make one's substantial achievements disappear.

STYLE AND FALSE ASSUMPTIONS

Why does virtually everyone believe, or act like they believe, that style is less important than the strength of one's achievements?

We have a stubborn faith in the meaningfulness of our achievements, because they are connected with our sense of self-worth. They are intimately associated with our identity, and they help make us feel good about ourselves. We consciously and unconsciously pursue this feeling. We will even disregard reality to protect how we think about ourselves. In the real world we can be awful at interviewing, and typically are. Yet, even though our continual failure to secure job offers is evidence of this fact, we will disregard it. If asked, "Are you a good or a bad interviewee?" The worst will tend to reply, "I'm above average."

This tendency toward self-delusion is part of the way we are psychologically wired.

> One of the most enduring lessons from social psychology is that…people go to great lengths to view the world in a way that maintains a sense of well-being. ….Just as we possess a potent physical immune system that protects us from threats to our physical well-being, so do we possess a potent psychological immune system that protects us from threats to our psychological well-being.[4]

Because of this immune system, we tend to focus on what makes us feel good about ourselves. This leads us to concentrate on our achievements and magnify their importance at the expense of style, or the manner in which we present them.

---

[4] Timothy D. Wilson, *Strangers to Ourselves: Discovering the Adaptive Unconscious* (Cambridge, MA: Belknap Press of Harvard University Press, 2002), p. 38.

There is another powerful reason to overlook matters of style, and it is also rooted in human nature. It takes a great deal of hard work to turn flat, lifeless answers into vibrant ones that resonate long after the interview. When Jack mentioned using stories, and having clear and concise answers, he failed to add, "And this takes weeks of hard work." I know it did. I worked with him to create them.

To avoid this time-consuming, difficult work, the vast majority of jobseekers take the easier path. They collect their achievements, great and small, and disgorge them during an interview, one data-point at a time. We are predisposed to seek this easy path:

> A general law of "least effort" applies to cognitive as well as physical exertion. The law asserts that if there are several ways of achieving the same goal, people will eventually gravitate to the least demanding course of action. In the economy of action, effort is a cost, and the acquisition of skill is driven by the benefits and costs. Laziness is built deep into our nature.[5]

This tendency, however, is not destiny, because "the acquisition of skill is driven by the *benefits* and costs." As I've found with most of my clients, once they understand the benefits of my approach they have the motivation and energy needed to acquire powerful job-search skills. So, one of the things I try to do is illumine the understanding of readers or audiences, about why a technique or practice is so important. I don't just say, "Write and remember clear and concise stories." I show you why it is absolutely essential to do this, and then show you how to do this. Because a poorly constructed story can do more harm than good as we shall see.

WHY THIS BOOK WAS WRITTEN

We have much to cover, but before we dive into this material, I'd like to share with you my personal motivation for providing this job search guide.

---

[5] Daniel Kahneman, *Thinking, Fast and Slow* (New York: Farrar, Straus and Giroux, 2011), p. 35. A great book that I highly recommend, though it is a dense, slow read.

I've coached thousands of jobseekers via radio—both as the interviewer and the interviewee—and through books I've written on the subject.[6] I've also taught hundreds through seminars for over fifteen years, coaching private clients and serving as a volunteer coach at the Career Transitions Center of Chicago (CTC).[7] The reason why I focus so much of my time on helping jobseekers is because I've experienced the anxiety and pain of being laid off. It can leave you feeling so hollowed out and empty that you can abandon hope.

I also know, firsthand, how ill-equipped most jobseekers are to do well at job search. Like virtually all of the jobseekers I meet, I was terrible at interviewing and networking, and blissfully ignorant about my incompetence. My psychological immune system led me to believe I was pretty good when I was awful.

I might never have discovered how badly I needed to improve in this area had I not received executive-outplacement assistance. It showed me I was doing almost everything wrong. But after mastering this new material I began to out-interview people who were far more qualified. I concluded, "This information is powerful. It could really help people."

I then developed and presented daylong, job-search seminars to those who were between jobs. I charged $50 for attending because offering it for free led to a large number of no-shows.

THE PATH TO JOB-SEARCH SUCCESS

Some time after this, I joined a corporation that manufactured and

---

[6] Two books, to be exact. This one and one entitled, *No Medal for Second Place: How to Finish First in Job Interviews*. This book that you are reading offers a more comprehensive and neuroscientific look at the subject of job search.
[7] The Center of Chicago is a place where I do volunteer coaching. If you are in the Chicago area you cannot possibly find a better job search value than the $300 program that the CTC offers. I believe it to be superior to executive outplacement programs that can easily cost more than twenty times as much. If you are not in the Chicago area they do offer virtual services as well. Their website is www.ctcchicago.org.

sold multi-million dollar communication systems through distributors. I was in charge of the sales department and saw how some of the distributors were good, but others were awful. In those parts of the country represented by good distributors, we did well. But we did poorly in the areas represented by woeful distributors, no matter how hard we supported them.

To remedy this situation, I developed a weeklong sales-training course to teach these distributors the art of complex sales. This forced me to think deeply about the sales process and the underlying psychological causes that led to the buying-decision-effect. This training program became a book, *The Causes of Sales Success*, that was favorably reviewed by one of the leading authorities on the subject of sales, Neil Rackham.[8]

Though we were a small, unknown company operating in a field of multi-billion dollar giants—Tyco, GE and Hill-Rom—who had polished, direct salespeople, we were able to grow to a greater than 50% market share.

I share this bit of background to let you know that the insights contained in this sales-training course are also a part of this book, and when I cover the oft-hated subject of sales, you will be thrilled with the news I will share. Namely, my system requires you to sell less than you are almost certainly doing in interviews right now. I will cover this in greater detail in the next chapter.

Finally, I also added the insights gained from my consultancy that uses information from fields as diverse as communication—verbal and non-verbal—neuroscience, creative problem solving, leadership, sales, and more. I think you will find much of this information new, fascinating and relevant to job search success.

BENEFITS

Among the long-term benefits that can be gained from this job search path are:

---

[8] Neil Rackham is the NY Times bestselling author of *Spin Selling*. When I cover the differences between simple and complex sales, these insights come from his groundbreaking work.

1. Understanding what makes you unique and defines the value you bring to any organization. And then leveraging the strengths you uncover at your next opportunity, making you more successful and engaged in your work.
2. Learning how to control the powerful, subconscious speech called non-verbal behavior. Its impact on communication is immense, and yet few focus on this area.
3. Learning how to communicate with stories, one of the most powerful uses of verbal communication.
4. Ways to improve your capacity to learn, think creatively, and much more.

In its early stages, the job-search path is often painful, but as you master the material in this book you will likely see how valuable this difficult education can be. It can teach you life-skills that will pave the way to even greater achievements.

In the next chapter we will look at the nature of the job-interviewing game, because until we know how to play the game, it is difficult to win.

2

The Nature of the Game

JOB SEARCH: HOW DIFFICULT CAN IT BE?

Job search is the most difficult game there is. There are many reasons why this is so. Here are a few of them:

1. It is a game that requires us to play in a certain way. However, human nature often programs us to act in the opposite way, as this chapter will continue to show.

2. Most jobseekers know that they are supposed to sell, or promote themselves, but they hate the idea of selling. How can anyone perform well at a task they despise?[1]

3. All jobseekers are selling, whether they want to or not, but virtually everyone of them has adopted the worst possible sales style, as I will soon illustrate.

4. Jobseekers are required to sell the most complex, hardest-to-sell product in the world—themselves. This is difficult because most people are uncomfortable promoting themselves.

---

[1] Whenever I ask a seminar audience to raise their hands if they enjoy interviewing very few hands are ever lifted.

5. Successful job search requires us to understand the value we represent, and then confidently express this value. But it is hard to be objective about ourselves. Most jobseekers struggle to understand what their strengths are for many weeks.

6. Jobseekers are required to sell this incredibly complex product under the most pressure-packed circumstance: the job interview. This isn't a seven-game series where you can lose three games and still advance. If you lose in the first round, bye-bye. You may have been a close second, but there is no medal for second place.

7. The job interview is a complex sale and few people—even salespeople—understand this approach.[2] Most jobseekers have never received an hour of training in the art of complex sales. Worse yet, there are few resources that do a good job covering this subject.

8. Finally, the game requires you to be upbeat and confident, even though you may have just received the leveling, painful blow of job loss.

Is there any wonder why most un-coached jobseekers, when they are handed the ball, take off in the wrong direction? Sending an untrained person to an interview is like taking someone who has never driven a car and giving them the keys, pointing out the location of the brakes, accelerator and steering wheel, and setting them free on the German autobahn for their maiden voyage. Godspeed!

GOOD NEWS FOR THOSE WHO HATE SELLING

The complex sales approach that you will learn from this book has the following great advantage: It does not feel like selling to either

---

[2] I'm sure they exist, but in my management positions in corporate America, and in my consulting assignments with other corporations, I've yet to find a salesperson who possessed all of the vital, complex-selling skills like differentiation, the use of stories, how to structure their presentations to their psychological advantage, etc.

you, or to the hiring authority. This is by design, because people love buying, but don't like being sold.

I remember taking a potential customer, and her team, to dinner, escorting them through a plant tour the next day, followed by our "sales presentation." We presented problems we had uncovered and their potential solutions. We spoke about their goals and how our product might lead to their achievement.

Lunch and a short walk to a waiting limo ended our time together. Before the buying authority entered the limo that was headed to O'Hare airport, she turned to me and said words I've never forgotten, "I've been with you for two days, and you've yet to try and sell me anything."

I smiled and said, "It's all my fault. Have a nice flight back home." But while I said that I thought, "I've been selling you from the moment you arrived." It did not feel that way, but she was sold. She did buy our system.

If you master this system you won't feel like you have been selling anyone, and that is just one of the many reasons why the system works. Remember, Jack was and is an engineer. Engineers tend not to like selling or have a strong urge to pursue a career in sales. Yet Jack adopted my approach and, as we will find out later, is still using some of its techniques to be successful in his new job.

MASTERING THE GAME

I hate golf and I can't understand why people take golfing vacations. I went to St. Andrews' University for my junior year abroad. It's the birthplace of golf. Golfers who learn of this always ask me, "Did you play on the Old Course?" Their eyes sparkle with delight, but their glimmer dies quickly when I answer, "Nope. Never even made it to the driving range or the putting green. But I did drink my fair share of pints at the Niblick." The Niblick is a pub that is very close to the Old Course.

What stands behind my aversion? I stink at golf. I don't like it and it doesn't like me. That is one of the reasons why people hate interviewing: They stink at it, and know this deep inside, even if they cannot consciously admit it to themselves.

If you seriously apply yourself to master the lessons in this book, then you will master the game of job search, and this can make interviewing enjoyable. I know this firsthand. I got to the point where I enjoyed interviewing. But I wanted to see if this was true for Jack, after two grueling days of eighteen interviews. His experience would be something of an acid test. So, I asked him if he enjoyed the experience and he replied:

> As far as the interviewing experience, surprisingly I did have a positive experience. I felt very prepared and felt confident that I could convey my experience and skills sets in a very effective manner (clear, concise and with stories).

Note how he continues to emphasize stylistic points like clarity, eliminating wordiness, and using stories. He learned valuable lessons about how to communicate effectively, and his continual repetition of these insights indicated he was not going to forget them.

Jack's experience reveals a key to job search success. We need to make the interviewing process enjoyable by mastering it, and by getting rid of our conventional, simple sales pitch.

THE SIMPLE SALE

Here is the crowning irony of job search: Those jobseekers who hate the idea of selling are unwittingly adopting the worst possible sales style. They typically use a simple sales approach that I will briefly describe so that it can be avoided at all costs.

In the simple sale there is typically one decision maker, because the price tag for the simple-sale's item, or service, is low. When the price is low, the risks of making a bad-buying decision are also low. If the decision maker purchases something that doesn't work out, his attitude is, "No big deal." He learns from his inexpensive mistake and moves on. For this reason there is no need to waste the time of multiple decision makers, or put a complex decision-making process in place. There is no committee making a buying decision in simple sales.

The simple sales approach looks like this:

> Salesperson: Hi, I'm Bill. I represent Acme, Inc., the ballpoint pen suppliers for most of the school systems in the state. The reason why we're twice as large as our next largest competitor is because of the quality of the product and the low cost. Most of my customers are placing their annual stocking orders right now, have you placed yours?
>
> Buyer: Nope.
>
> Salesperson: So how many pens do you need to fill your stocking order? [Followed by...] That order would cost _____. If you place your order now you can get free shipping and it will arrive by next week. Deal?
>
> Buyer: Maybe. I'll think about it.
>
> Salesperson: That's fine. But if you think about it, you've got a hundred more important things to think about. How about we take this item off your to-do list and get you set up for the school year with the best quality pens at a discounted price?
>
> Buyer: You're probably right. Use this P.O. number.

I rattle off a few of the most impressive facts and then I close, close, close. Ask for the order! If an objection arises, I answer it and then close, close, close. However, in the complex sales process I never asked for the order. Not once, much less three times.

Now let's apply this simple sales approach to the job interview to see what it looks like.

THE SIMPLE JOB INTERVIEW

The simple sales style can work during an interview, but only for a simple job opportunity. These are the low-skilled, low-paying jobs where one person meets the candidate and often makes the hiring decision on the spot. The downside of making a bad decision is low so no hiring committee is ever formed.

Take, for example, a dishwashing job. The interview might go like this:

Kitchen Manager: You here for the dishwashing job?

Interviewee: Yep.

Kitchen Manager: We pay the minimum wage and the hours are Tuesday through Saturday night, from five in the evening to one in the morning.

Interviewee: Cool. I work hard and show up on time. Do I start tonight?

Offer a few *reasons* why you should be hired and ask for the job. This is a very direct and *rational* approach, and for the simple job opportunity this makes sense. The hiring authority is exposed to little risk if he makes a bad decision. If things don't pan out, then another warm body can quickly be found. Emotion will only enter the equation when the stakes are higher, the compensation and responsibilities are greater, and it becomes a higher-risk, higher-reward decision. Then the process becomes more complex. Several people interview multiple candidates, and the "sale" is no longer simple.

JOBSEEKERS SELLING POORLY

Unfortunately, this rational, simple sales approach is adopted by almost all of my clients prior to seeing me. They interview as if driven by this philosophy: *Whoever presents the most reasons, and the best reasons, will win the interviewing contest.*

Whether they've thought about it or not, they act like the hiring decision is a rational one. After all, how could something so important to their life and career be irrational? "Doesn't the hiring authority want to hire the best?" their thought process goes. "And don't I need to show them I am the best by piling up the evidence that this is so?"

If the interviewer was a computer that could hear every reason why we are the best candidate, immediately calculate its worth, and simultaneously compare these weighted reasons to those of the other four candidates, then they would choose us if our qualifications outweighed our competition's. But the hiring authority is human—most of the time—and he can't keep up with weighing the information, organizing it, remembering it, etc., before more arrives.

Now multiply the impact of this data-dumping style times five (you and your four competitors). By the end of the fifth interview, the hiring authority's ears are bleeding and his head is about to explode. He forgets what has been said and who said it. The continuous stream of facts and data creates a data fog, and all of the candidates disappear in it. The exhausted interviewer struggles to associate resumes with the people he met mere hours ago.

THE CAUSES OF THE HIRING-DECISION-EFFECT

This rational, simple-sales approach doesn't work, because the complex hiring decision is caused by emotions, not reasons. If we are to cause a hiring decision, then we need to employ these emotional causes.

Let's compare the hiring of dishwashers to the hiring of professionals. With dishwashers there was a low risk-reward element in the decision. But when it comes to hiring professionals, a higher risk-reward relationship is in play.

If, for example, I hire a disruptive person for my marketing team, someone who destroys my team's chemistry and is disrespectful to authority figures, then I have not only made my life miserable, but I've hurt the productivity of the team, my company and my standing within it. I will now appear to be a poor judge of character and an ineffective team builder. Conversely, when I hire someone who exceeds all expectations, it makes my life easier as a manager, and it reflects well on me.

The risk and reward of hiring professionals introduces emotion into the decision-making process. I *fear* making a mistake. I don't hire someone who I cannot *trust*, or who makes me *feel uncomfortable*. I hire people I *like* and who I *want* to be around.

PERCEPTION AND EMOTION

One of the reasons why emotions cause hiring decisions is because they shape perception. Favorable emotions can create a filter that keeps the hiring authority from seeing our weaknesses, while negative feelings can keep them from seeing our strengths. For example, when our interviewing style gets an interviewer to like us, this influences their perception in ways that favor us, because "perception is affected not only by what people *expect* to see; it is also colored by what they *want* to see."[3]

The hiring authority looks for reasons to hire the candidate they like the most. They begin to see "what they *want* to see." When candidates are liked, then everything they say or do is colored in a positive way. There is a psychological reason why love is blind: We see what we want to see.

Let's return to the woman who said I had yet to sell her anything. She did not realize that the reason why we took her and her team up to the top of the Hancock Building for drinks, then out to a nice dinner, was to generate positive feelings toward us. Then, when we made our presentation, we did not present facts and data, but solutions to problems that caused painful feelings. In short, I was using emotions to cause the buying-decision-effect.

Once we understand the importance of emotion we will take a less rational approach to our quest for employment. We will stop focusing on the limited rational mind, and will make our appeal to another mental system that is more emotional. This emotional system will make its debut in the next chapter. The way it impacts decision-making, communication, and perception will change our job-search course.

---

[3] Scott Plous, *The Psychology of Judgment and Decision Making* (New York: McGraw Hill, 1993), p. 18.

3

Who's Running the Show?

DECISION-MAKING

Are we in control of our decisions? We consciously make them, so it would appear we are, but researchers are discovering surprising things about the way our mind works. Take, for example, how people form impressions of others, a psychological process important to jobseekers as they network and interview.

John Bargh and Paula Pietromonaco conducted an experiment to see if non-conscious information might shape our perception of someone. They asked the participants to tell them if the flash on the computer screen came from the right or left of the screen. What the participants did not know was the flash contained a word. Since these words appeared for only a tenth of a second, and were followed by a line of x's, the conscious mind was unaware of a word being shown. But another mental system took note.

> In one condition, 80 percent of the words had to do with hostility, such as "hostile," "insult," and "unkind." In a second condition, none of the words had to do with hostility. Next, people took part in what they thought was an unrelated experiment on how people form impressions of others. They read a paragraph describing a man named Donald, who acted in somewhat ambiguous ways that

might be construed as hostile, such as, "A salesman knocked at the door, but Donald refused to let him enter."

Those who had seen flashes of hostile words judged Donald to be more hostile and unfriendly than did people who had not seen the flashes of hostile words...."[1]

Who is in control? Is it our rational, conscious self? In the above experiment the rational, conscious mind did not come to its conclusions independently. Its perception was shaped by non-conscious information. This points to the existence of another mental system operating outside of our conscious awareness that influences the conclusions people make about others.

Decisions are made by the rational mind, but not without being influenced by a mental system that is subconscious and more emotional. When we understand how these two mental systems operate—one conscious and one subconscious—it will point to changes we need to make in our job search practices. The mere exposure effect illustrates the operation of these two systems and some of the changes we should make.

THE MERE EXPOSURE EFFECT

Our minds are wired to view novelty as a threat, but repetition of this novel stimulus can eventually make it acceptable and good in our estimation. This psychological mechanism appears to be tied to our survival fitness.

Roger Zajonc, a prominent researcher in this field, "argued that the effect of repetition on liking is a profoundly important biological fact, and it extends to all animals. To survive in a frequently dangerous world, an organism should react cautiously to a novel stimulus, with withdrawal and fear. Survival prospects are poor for an animal that is not suspicious of novelty. However, it is also adaptive for the initial caution to fade if the stimulus is actually safe. The mere exposure effect occurs, Zajonc claimed, because the repeated exposure of a stimulus is followed by nothing bad."[2]

---

[1] Timothy D. Wilson, p. 30.
[2] Kahneman, p. 67.

The following experiment illustrates the impact of the mere exposure effect. Researchers placed an ad box on the front page of a university newspaper and each day it had a Turkish sounding word in it. Sometimes the word was "ikitaf," while other times it was "saricik," "kadirga," "nansoma," and "biwonjni." One of these words appeared twenty-five times, while the others only appeared ten, five, two or one time.

After the words stopped appearing members in the university community received questionnaires asking which words were good or bad. The words appearing more frequently were rated more favorably than the words appearing only once or twice. This experiment has been replicated using faces, polygons, and Chinese characters.

Rationally speaking, these made-up words were neither good nor bad, but a subconscious part of the experimental subject's minds thought otherwise, and it influenced their conscious minds to select some words as being good and others as being bad. And like the previous experiment with the flashing words, the mere exposure effect is in operation even when the words are shown so quickly on a computer screen that the observers are unaware they've seen them. Those words that are repeated more frequently to our subconscious mind appear to be good to our conscious mind.

Who's running this show, anyway?

We are, to a certain degree, but it is not without our conscious decisions being heavily influenced by subconscious processes. And as we start to understand how our mind works we can begin to modify job search practices. For example, repetition needs to be a part of our job search strategy. We need to intentionally repeat key themes with our branding statements, stories and answers to typical questions. These themes will be repeated again in our resume, cover letter, and follow-up correspondence.

Repetition is powerful. If you want someone to believe a lie, keep repeating it. Dictators successfully use this technique. But the reverse is also true. If you want the truth about who you are, and the value you represent, to be believed, then repeat it. In effect, you are creating patterns in the subconscious mind of the interviewer that will remain there, long after the interview, exerting a favorable influence on the conscious decisions the interviewer eventually must make. The emotion of fear toward novelty is being replaced with the feeling of comfort toward familiarity. However, repetition requires variation to make it work in the interview. Saying the exact same thing twenty-five times during an hour-long interview will not generate favorable results.

ONE MIND, TWO MENTAL SYSTEMS

Our mind has at least two mental systems. One of them is called the cognitive unconscious, the adaptive unconscious, or System 1. It is more emotional, always on and very fast. The rational, conscious mind—System 2—is only on when we are awake and it is slow. According to one researcher, the cognitive unconscious processes 11,000,000 bits of sensory data per second, while the rational mind processes about 40 bits per second.[3]

The rational mind has beliefs, makes choices and plans, and can perform complex computations like 89 X 34 = ____. The cognitive unconscious is not very good at math, but it can handle a simple math problem like 2 + 2 = ___. It has an association for that computation that it readily supplies. You don't even have to think about the answer. It is an associative machine, and it is effortless in its operation.

The cognitive unconscious is always scanning the horizon for threats, because it is programmed to keep us alive and healthy. It makes our responses to potential threats—like novelty—automatic and instantaneous.

To carry out this mission it maintains our internal map of the world. Without it we would not be able to recognize these threats. For example, in this map are the many facial expressions we encounter everyday, and each expression has an appropriate

---

[3] "Scientists have determined this number [11,000,000—my note] by counting the receptor cells each sense organ has and the nerves that go from these cells to the brain. Our eyes alone receive and send over 10,000,000 signals to our brains each second." From: Timothy D. Wilson, p. 24.

emotion associated with it. When a person approaches you with an angry facial expression you immediately know he is angry. His tone of voice and body language can also instantly communicate this to you.

When the cognitive unconscious recognizes a potential threat it communicates this to our rational mind through our body. An uneasy feeling shouts, "This person bears watching!" This feeling is in part caused by physiological changes. You did not request a jolt of epinephrine to be released into your blood stream, nor were you asked for permission.[4] It happened independently of your conscious control.

There was no logical thought process that went, "His face is slightly reddened, eyes are blazingly intense, tone is edgy, body language is aggressive and belligerent, therefore, based on past experiences, this suggests that he is angry. Angry people can act irrationally and violently. I do not know this person. This makes this stranger a threat. I'd better prepare to fight or run."

If our minds worked this slowly we would have been an extinct species a long time ago. To survive we needed to recognize and respond to threats immediately, before they overtook us. Our cognitive unconscious sounded alarm bells immediately upon seeing the angry face, and prepared our body to fight or fly.

During seminars I sometimes say, "The following is an act." I then make an angry face and walk toward someone close by with my finger pointing toward their face and growl, "We ... need ... to talk!" I then ask, "Did you feel anything?"

The last time I did this a woman said, "Like I was going to throw up!" I apologized and said, "But your rational mind was told, 'This is just an act.' And you are in a safe place. Your fear of me makes no rational sense, but this doesn't matter to the cognitive unconscious. It took over and activated the flight-or-fight response without asking for your permission."

---

[4] We call the glands that produce adrenaline our adrenal glands. But in the U.S. physicians use the word *epinephrine* in place of *adrenaline*. This makes sense, doesn't it?

We automatically and instantly evaluate, and respond to, non-verbal behaviors like facial expressions, tone of voice and body language. So do interviewers. This requires jobseekers to master non-verbal communication, because during an interview our non-verbal behavior is continually communicating a message to the cognitive unconscious of the interviewer. Unfortunately, much of the time it is the wrong message. We will learn more about the nature and power of non-verbal behavior in the coming chapters.

OUR UNCONSCIOUS MISGUIDANCE SYSTEM

Our powerful desire to feel good about ourselves can make us sacrifice accuracy, or the truth, for the sake of this good feeling. To rationalize a bad outcome, and make it more palatable, a jobseeker might *consciously* think, "I failed to get the job because the interviewer felt threatened by my credentials. He didn't want to hire his replacement." This rationalization keeps him from the painful truth that he needs to work hard to improve his interviewing style. So, he continues to make the same mistakes as he moves in the wrong direction down the job search path.

Compounding the power of this psychological immune system, and its ability to mislead us, is the way it works subconsciously.

> Given that the adaptive unconscious plays a major role in selecting, interpreting, and evaluating incoming information, though, it is no surprise that one of the rules it follows is "Select, interpret, and evaluate information in ways that make me feel good." Furthermore, there is reason to believe that the adaptive unconscious is a better spin doctor than the conscious mind.[5]

Who is running this show? We are not only consciously steering ourselves in the wrong direction, we are unconsciously doing so, and this aspect of our nature affects job search.

One of my clients at the Career Transitions Center of Chicago was a technically brilliant person whose mind could quickly solve some of the most complex, technical problems, but he was failing in

---

[5] Timothy D. Wilson, p. 39

interview after interview. This angered him and he was completely unaware that his emotions were starting to get the best of him.

During one session he angrily snapped at me for the gentlest modification of an answer. I explained the need for modifying it and eventually he could see the point. Later he described how he was getting angry at the stupidity of the hiring authorities for not being able to see what a great candidate he was, and he was using his anger to give him energy. He said this as if it was a good idea.

To feel good about his interviewing failures he was creating the narrative that the hiring authorities were the problem because they were stupid. Little did he realize how he was the problem. He was unconsciously sacrificing accuracy about what the real problem was to both feel good about himself, and to justify his negative emotions. He was blissfully unaware of how his anger was bubbling to the surface. His bristling behavior was ending interviews before they began.

The war we must win is fought within. The psychological immune system is part of this war that is being waged:

> The conflict between the need to be accurate and the desire to feel good about ourselves is one of the major battlegrounds of the self, and how this battle is waged and how it is won, are central determinants of who we are and how we feel about ourselves.[6]

TAKING CONTROL

What are we to do? This psychological defense mechanism was created not to harm us but to help us, and it will continue to operate whether we want it to or not. Knowing this, we need to adopt an approach that prevents some of its harmful effects.

We need to make "continuous improvement" a guiding principle of job search. This principle does not condemn us for poor performances, or congratulate us for excellent ones. Instead, it looks at both performances and says, "I could have done better.

---

[6] Timothy D. Wilson, p. 39

Now I need to look at all aspects of my job search and figure out what are the most important improvements that I can make."

Our stories can be made better, so we subject them to another round of editing. The delivery of our stories can be made better, so we rehearse more. Our networking can improve, so we review our plan and approach.

To keep from fighting against human nature, we do not activate our psychological immune system by looking at the bad, the failures, and so on. Instead, we focus on making things better.

This mirrors the approach I use when coaching someone. The first part of my critique covers what they are doing right. I want to create a safe place for criticism. To some extent this praise disarms the psychological immune system. Then, instead of criticism, I offer a possible improvement and ask them what they think. The result is, more often than not, behavioral change, the adoption of a success behavior or the removal of a harmful one.

By being accurate about our situation we move toward a time when we will feel much better about ourselves, namely, when we are employed.

THE NEXT STEP

In the next chapter we will look at the effect two mental states have on our performance, as we continue to align our job search practices with human nature. They reveal another way we are often unknowingly sabotaging ourselves.

4

Cognitive Ease, Cognitive Strain, and Clarity

COGNITIVE EASE AND STRAIN

Two mental states—cognitive ease and cognitive strain—affect the way people process information. Understanding these two mental states is important, because one works for the jobseeker and the other works against him.

When the rational mind is called into action a state of cognitive strain exists, and there are things that automatically move this conscious mind to act. For example, novelty triggers cognitive strain, because it is perceived to be a potential threat. The cognitive unconscious sends the suggestion, "Rational mind, attend to this! This is new! It does not appear anywhere in my map of the world." Cognitive strain "indicates that a problem exists, which will require increased mobilization of System 2."[1]

A state of cognitive ease exists when "things are going well—no threats, no major news, no need to redirect attention or mobilize effort."[2] Repetition can lead to cognitive ease. The novel stimulus

---

[1] Kahneman, p. 59. System 2 is the rational, conscious mind
[2] Kahneman, p. 59.

has become familiar and safe, and the rational mind can go back to resting, which is what it prefers to do.

We want to use an interviewing style that keeps the rational mind of the interviewer at rest, or at ease, because:

> When you feel strained, you are more likely to be *vigilant and suspicious*, invest more effort in what you are doing, *feel less comfortable*, and make fewer errors, but you also are less intuitive, less creative than usual.[3]

We don't want the interviewer to be "vigilant and suspicious" while we are interviewing. The cognitive unconscious moves the rational mind to action, because it senses a problem or threat exists. The rational mind then critically analyzes the situation to see what is wrong instead of accepting what it sees and hears. Cognitive strain biases the mind toward doubt and skepticism.

Just as bad, cognitive strain makes the interviewer feel uncomfortable. Who hires someone who makes them feel uncomfortable? Only the desperate, confused, or crazy.

Cognitive ease has the opposite effect:

> When you are in a state of cognitive ease, you are probably in a good mood, like what you see, *believe what you hear*, trust your intuitions, and feel that the current situation is comfortably familiar.[4]

Cognitive ease biases the mind toward belief just as cognitive strain biases the mind toward disbelief. So, how do you create cognitive ease and steer clear of cognitive strain?

CAUSES OF COGNITIVE STRAIN AND EASE

Among the causes of cognitive ease, noted by Kahneman, is repetition, which we've covered. Another cause is clarity. George Orwell illustrates how much more powerful language is when it is simple and direct, compared to its unclear counterpart:

---

[3] Kahneman, p. 60. My emphasis.
[4] Kahneman, p. 60. My emphasis.

I am going to translate a passage of good English into modern English of the worst sort. Here is a well-known verse from *Ecclesiastes*:

> I returned and saw under the sun, that the race is not to the swift, nor the battle to the strong, neither yet bread to the wise, nor yet riches to men of understanding, nor yet favour to men of skill; but time and chance happeneth to them all.

Here it is in modern English:

> Objective consideration of contemporary phenomena compels the conclusion that success or failure in competitive activities exhibits no tendency to be commensurate with innate capacity, but that a considerable element of the unpredictable must invariably be taken into account.[5]

The "modern English" example's lack of clarity makes our rational minds spring into action to decode this gibberish. It causes cognitive strain. Therefore, we must strive for simplicity in our speech.

READABILITY

The clarity of our scripted response to the "tell me about yourself" question, or other scripted answers, can be objectively measured. The "Spelling and Grammar" tool in the Microsoft Word program, for Macs and PCs, can tell us whether or not our branding statements, or other responses, are clear and easy to read.[6]

---

[5] George Orwell, *The Penguin Essays of George Orwell* (London: Penguin Books Ltd, 1984), p. 359.

[6] For Macs, simply click "Tools," click "Spelling and Grammar." Once you are finished checking the spelling and grammar it will automatically display some readability statistics.

However, if you are highlighting only a portion of a Word document it will ask you if you want to continue checking the rest of the document. Click "No," because you are only interested in the readability score for the highlighted portion of the document. It then shows you statistics that

One of these readability measurements is the Flesch-Kincaid Grade Level. Articles in the Wall Street Journal tend to average an 8th-10th-grade level. Novels by John Grisham are around a 7th-8th-grade level. Your branding statement and stories should be in this 6th-9th-grade range. If it is higher than this, then shorten your sentences, simplify the sentence structure, and replace larger words with smaller words.

The above quote from Ecclesiastes has a Flesch-Kincaid Grade Level of 8.4. As for Orwell's Modern English example, it achieves the highest grade level of this scale, which is 12.[7]

The "Spelling and Grammar" statistics also give you a Flesch Reading Ease score. The score of "0" is impenetrable. The score of sixty or higher fits into the category of "Plain English." It means a thirteen-year-old student can easily understand this writing. A score of sixty or higher is what we should aim for.

The quote from Ecclesiastes is very easy to read: 78.3. The Modern English example is the first writing sample I've come across that scores "0," a score it richly deserves. The Harvard Law Review scores in the low thirties. (This entire book is above 60.)

It helps to have an objective assessment of our clarity, because most people are not objective about their own writing. Just remember, the clearer your message is, the more it causes the hiring authority to remain at cognitive ease, a mental state biased toward belief.

---

indicate the clarity level of our writing.
It also works on Word for PCs, and how to access this feature on a PC appears in the next footnote.

[7] This readability feedback also works for Word documents on PCs, but accessing this feature takes a few more steps. This comes from Microsoft Office Support: Click File, Click Options. Click Proofing. Under **When correcting spelling and grammar in Word** make sure the **Check grammar with spelling** check box is selected. Select **Show readability statistics.** After you enable the feature, open a file that you want to check and *check the spelling*. When Word finishes checking the spelling and grammar, it displays information about the reading level of the document.

I use these clarity assessment tools to help me assess my own work, and the work of clients. It helps both of us to see the need of simplifying our work to make it clearer.

CLARITY: MORE DIFFICULT THAN IT SEEMS

Clarity is a problem area for many of my clients, because it is hard work developing clear and concise answers to an interviewer's questions. It involves writing a first draft of an answer to a typical question, and then editing it and re-editing it many times. That is a lot of work for one answer, and this exercise must be repeated many times to prepare for other questions.

As the excellent prose stylist, William Zinsser, noted in his book, *On Writing Well*:

> …Writing is hard work. A *clear sentence* is no accident. Very few sentences come out right the first time, or even the third time. …If you find that writing is hard, it's because it is hard. It is one of the hardest things that people do.[8]

When Mr. Zinsser writes about writing being hard, he means writing effectively is hard. It is the same thing with writing stories. I've given many workshops on developing this skill. One student once commented, "Writing stories is easy." True. But writing effective stories is not.

IT'S TOUGH EVEN FOR ENGLISH MAJORS

A client of mine, named Tess, is good with words and very smart. She should be. She has a degree in English from a fine liberal arts college, Wellesley, and an MBA from the University of Chicago, one of the top MBA programs in the country.

Like many people in the workforce her career experienced a little turbulence during the aftershocks of the Great Recession. To

---

[8] William Zinsser, *On Writing Well: An Informal Guide to Writing Non-Fiction* (New York: Harper & Row, Publishers, Inc., 1985), p. 12. My emphasis.

remove any concerns a hiring authority might have about the spottiness of her recent track record, she wrote a story.

Imagine Tess being interviewed and being asked, "Recently you seem to have a pretty spotty track record. Would you help me understand what happened?" Tess could answer with her story:

> I understand your concern. I had short stints at Acme Media and The Acme, unfortunately.[9] Both of them were small digital companies and changed strategies after six months to remain competitive and respond to market conditions, leading to layoffs. I was drawn to them because the people in the companies were very smart, the product seemed innovative, and I like being part of a team that builds a business. But the downside of a start up is that resources are limited and if they decide to change direction and want to free up revenue, they'll cut headcount.
>
> My last three sales jobs have all involved helping clients use data to help advertisers make more impactful and effective ad campaigns, and are great experience for working at Acmecom, to help clients use business intelligence to generate marketing insights.
>
> I have been successful in companies which experienced rapid change and growth, specifically [at a well-known web business], where I worked for five years during a volatile period of digital advertising. Given this volatility I want to make sure that my next company has a great road map and strong management in place to direct it.

When I received this story I checked to see how readable it was. The Reading Ease score was lower than it should have been (48.7), and the grade level was as high as it could be (grade 12).

I then spoke with Tess on the phone and said, "Tess, you know this story better than anyone, because you wrote it. What I'd like to do is read it to you. I want you to be the interviewer, and I am you addressing my recent, spotty track record. Okay?"

---

[9] These were the last two companies appearing on her resume.

I read it to her and asked, "Were you able to follow it easily, or did it lose you in places." Tess said, "It kind of lost me in places."

"I thought it might," I replied, "because it had that effect on me. When something is unclear the rational mind is called into action to try and decipher what is being said. This leads to cognitive strain. Cognitive strain biases the interviewer's mind toward doubt. As the interviewer struggles to understand your story, he also begins to doubt it. Something doesn't feel right about it. It's like you are hiding something.

"Now I'd like for you to hear an edited version and see what you think." I then read her an edited version of her story:

> I understand your concern. I was drawn to these two start-ups, Acme Media and The Acme, because they had innovative products. I also wanted to be part of a team that builds a business.
>
> But start-ups change strategies more quickly than other organizations. They both decided to go in a different direction after about six months. Their resources were limited, so they reduced headcount to free up revenue. And I was among the many who were let go.
>
> To keep this from happening again, I am seeking an opportunity with an established, growing company. I worked for five years at a company like that. It was [a well-known web business] and I posted some of the best results in the company. I am looking forward to repeating that success.

I asked her if that was easier to follow and, even though she was the author of the first story, my edited version was clearer, even to her.

What about the reading ease score? It went from 48.7 to 63.8. It was now in the plain English category. And as for grade level it went from the highest, 12th grade, to a 7th grade level—7.2, to be exact.

Now, as Tess uses this story during an interview, the clarity of it leads to cognitive ease. The sensibility of it raises no red flags. The interviewer's mind, biased toward belief, would likely accept her answer and move on.

When we get to the section on verbal behavior we will look at stories in great detail. One of the things that make them so powerful is the way they are familiar. If you start to tell a good story, the conscious, rational mind relaxes and a new narrative pattern lodges in the cognitive unconscious to assert its influence long after the interview.

THE ACQUISITION OF LIFE SKILLS

Though this path requires effort, I am hopeful that you will be a motivated student who sees the value of this work. What you are working on are life skills that will help you succeed in job search, and in whatever job you eventually land. For example, the skill of developing stories is something that is being taught to the highest executives at the largest corporations in the world.

> Today, many of the most successful organizations on the planet intentionally use storytelling as a key leadership tool: Nike…3M…Berkshire Hathaway…Disney, Costco….
>
> At Nike, *all* the senior executives are designated "corporate storytellers." Several companies actively teach storytelling skills to their leaders. Kimberly-Clark, for example, has held two-day seminars to teach its 13-step program for crafting a story and structuring presentations using them.[10]

Communicating through stories works in interviews and in life.

RATIONAL, SIMPLE SALES AND COGNITIVE STRAIN

I want you to experience, in a very limited manner, a different type of cognitive strain that interviewers routinely feel. They ask the

---

[10] Paul Smith, *Lead With a Story: A Guide to Crafting Business Narratives that Captivate, Convince and Inspire* (New York: AMACOM Books, 2012), pp. 2-3. This book is good for business people, but its way of structuring stories is not effective for job interviews. His format is too lengthy and, with its twists and turns, is not as clear and direct as the one you will be taught.

question, "Will you tell me about yourself?" and the jobseeker is fully prepared to "wow" them with his greatness. Unclear language is not required to create cognitive strain. All that is needed is a continual flow of achievements, a regurgitation of the many things that make this jobseeker feel good about himself:

> I received both academic and swimming scholarships from twelve universities. But I chose Superlative University because of the reputation of their business courses. While there, I was a gold medalist in the State tournaments every year. My dad was an Olympic swimmer so I guess it runs in the family. I graduated magna cum laude. After graduation I received multiple job offers. Ultimately I decided that Acme, Inc. was the best fit. My initial position was managing a production line of twenty union employees. I instituted a six-sigma quality program. Over a four-year period the overall quality improvement was 50%. I also have excellent performance reviews covering every year I worked at Acme...

And this blowhard is still on his very first job!

Our rational minds prefer rest, or cognitive ease. A deluge of data forces our rational mind to wake up and process it all. But, as mentioned before, we are humans and not computers. We can't process the data deluge fast enough.

In the above example, some of the data is very meaningful to the interviewee, but of little interest to the interviewer unless it is made so. The interviewer is likely thinking, "He's a gold-medal-winning swimmer. Okay. Great. But he's not going to be swimming in this job."

The interviewer's mind struggles to keep up until it finally checks out. His eyes are open, but his mind is on a beach in Mexico.

The data-dump is an illustration of someone who is selling too hard. It feels like selling, bad selling, to both parties. It offers proud features, but few benefits. It has a boastful tone that does little to make a candidate likable. In fact, this can alienate the interviewer, especially when his achievements don't compare. His psychological immune system, always working to protect his feelings about himself, may kick into gear and produce thoughts like, "This guy sure thinks highly of himself. He probably thinks he's better than me. I wonder if he will think that when he doesn't make it to the next round." This is not the impression we want to make.

CLARIFICATION HELPS US UNDERSTAND

We cannot be clear about something that is unclear to us. Most jobseekers are confused about what they've achieved, and/or what their strengths are (more on that topic in the chapter, *Self-Discovery*). They tend to diminish aspects of their accomplishments that are noteworthy, or they forget them. This makes the clear recounting of their achievements to an interviewer an impossible task.

To remedy this, write down answers to the typical interviewing questions and edit each one several times. With each editing pass the value you are trying to convey comes into sharper focus. The first time you wrote down an answer to the, "What are your strengths question," you probably had a rambling mess of an answer. As you edited your answer to clarify it, your strengths became clearer. Your next editing pass might have introduced a new, powerful element that you had forgotten about. Pretty soon you will have an answer that is clear and compelling.

The difficulty of producing clear answers and stories is one of the biggest obstacles on the path to job search success. As I've told numerous audiences, "If I was to pick the single most important thing that separates those who are successful in their job search from those who are not, it is the way the successful ones work hard on the right things. For example, they work hard on developing an authentic voice that delivers well-crafted stories, a clear and concise branding statement, and other answers. Their authentic voice wins interviews and generates networking momentum. People are compelled to hire and to help the person who speaks this way, because they want to."

WHERE THE PATH LEADS NEXT

We've studied some important subjects that are, at first, counter-intuitive. For example, we tend to focus on the substance of our accomplishments instead of the way we word them. This leads to substantial achievements vanishing in the fog of a data-dump, or in unclear sentences.

We've also learned about the nature of the "sale." It is an emotional sale, not a rational one. Therefore, the way we present ourselves needs to generate emotions like trust, warmth, comfort, hope and likability.

Our amazing mind is so complex that we are only beginning to understand how it operates. Nonetheless, our rudimentary knowledge provides enough insight to change how we present ourselves. There are ways to modify our style so that it works with our two mental systems instead of against them.

These insights are helping us to change our course and start running in the right direction. This course change will continue, but now it will focus on the non-verbal component of speech, or the way we deliver our words.

Our facial expression, tone of voice and body language communicate to the interviewer's cognitive unconscious in powerful ways that can determine the outcome of the interview in less than one minute. The interviewer may think he is making a conscious decision in choosing us or not choosing us, and he is.

However, it is a decision that is heavily influenced by suggestions coming from the cognitive unconscious, of which he is unaware. Non-verbal behaviors generate many of these powerful suggestions. For this reason, the next four chapters are dedicated to gaining control of our non-verbal voice.

PART 2:

MASTERING NON-VERBAL COMMUNICATION

5

The Power of Non-Verbal Behaviors

THE COMMUNICATION PROBLEM

Bill really wanted this job. His financial position was wobbly, and he feared what might happen if he failed to get the offer. As he sat in the lobby waiting for ten agonizing minutes he struggled to calm himself. He thought, "It's natural to be nervous." Then he thought, "Natural, but not good," and his nervousness increased.

Joan, from Human Resources, came down to fetch him. He stood up, unconsciously wiped a sweaty palm against his pants leg, and shook hands. He tried to smile and look relaxed, but his poor attempt at acting only made him feel worse. He followed Joan down a long, endless hallway and then slumped in his chair. He looked more like a man facing a firing squad, than the most desirable candidate in the pool of interviewees. He looked like this because he felt like this.

As Joan asked questions he struggled to breathe deeply and maintain eye contact. His facial expression was tense and pale. The tone of his voice had a higher pitch than normal, and his movements were stiff. His verbal message was fine, but his non-verbal behaviors undermined everything he was trying to say.

Then, about ten minutes into the interview, he began to relax and regain his voice, but by then it was too late. Joan's cognitive unconscious was sounding a loud alarm, "He's not the one! Next!" and her conscious mind accepted this suggestion. Bill failed to make the final cut.

It's so unfair. Why should anyone be disregarded after a few minutes, or less? Because, as we will see, that is the way we are wired. We can argue against human nature, but we cannot make it go away. Our only hope for success is to align our job search actions with it. This requires that we understand mindsets, because they shape perception and can work for us or against us.

Mindsets have the following characteristics: They are quick to form, resist change, and assimilate all additional information to conform to the existing image.[1] They shape the path our mind goes down as you are about to experience.

MINDSETS

What do you see?

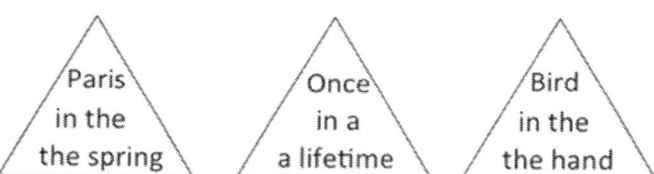

Most people see, "Paris in the spring, "Once in a lifetime," and, "Bird in the hand." Only it doesn't say that. It says, "Paris in *the the* spring,' "Once in *a a* lifetime," and "Bird in *the the* hand."

Our minds are perceptually wired to see the familiar phrase that we expect to see, not the phrase that is actually there. We filter out the extra word so that the statement fits the preexisting phrase in our head.

---

[1] Richards J. Heuer, Jr., *Psychology of Intelligence Analysis,* (Center for the Study of Intelligence, CIA, 1999), pp. 10, 11. This book is now out of print and this quote comes from a pdf that is available at www.odci.gov/csi.

Many people say, "Perception is reality," though it isn't. Reality is "Paris in the the spring." That's what *really* is there, but this reality is not what people typically perceive. In some ways perception is more important and powerful than reality, because reality frequently submits to it.

The above image of "Paris in the the spring" is referred to as "Figure 1" in the following quote:

> Did you perceive Figure 1 correctly? If so, you have exceptional powers of observation, were lucky, or have seen the figure before. This simple experiment demonstrates one of the most fundamental principles concerning perception:
>
> **We tend to perceive what we expect to perceive.**[2]

Mindsets are like a subconscious expectation to see something that is then seen, even though it doesn't exist. The mindset that is fairly easy to recognize and understand is a first impression. If you favorably impress me when I first meet you, then I interpret everything you continue to do or say in a favorable light. I rationalize your stutters, stumbles and misstatements. My first impression formed quickly, is resisting change, and is assimilating all conflicting data to fit my first impression. I now expect to see you in a certain way, and I do.

DO YOU CONTROL MINDSETS?

Mindsets are inevitable and outside of our control. We cannot prevent them from forming in our minds, and even when we are aware of them, it is extremely difficult to resist their influence.

The CIA knows this. The above image of the three triangles, and "Paris in the the Spring," comes from a CIA book entitled, *The Psychology of Intelligence Analysis*. Even though their analysts are taught about the influence of mindsets, they are still not immune to their influence.

Take the Second Iraq War as an example. This was a highly

---

[2] Heuer, p. 8. His emphasis, not mine.

controversial war that was opposed by France, Germany and Russia. These nations thought the war was a bad idea, but they did not disagree with the U.S. intelligence assessments that Iraq possessed weapons of mass destruction (WMD).

There was only one small problem with this intelligence community's consensus about Iraqi WMDs: They did not exist; only the mindset that Iraq had them did.

This mindset was probably the result of Saddam Hussein's past use of chemical weapons on the Kurdish population in Iraq. The intelligence community's thinking might have traveled down this path: "No sociopathic dictator like Hussein would ever give up one of his most powerful weapons. We know he had them at one time, because we have proof he used them. Therefore, he still must have them." Only he didn't. Evidence that went against this mindset was rationalized, or filtered out, as the mindset resisted change and assimilated all incoming information to fit the preexisting image.

THE FIRST FEW SECONDS

A 1993 study by Nalini Ambady and Robert Rosenthal illustrates how we can quickly and accurately evaluate people after seeing only a few seconds of non-verbal behavior. They took videotapes of entire class sessions from thirteen teachers and extracted three ten-second video clips from them, and then removed the sound track. Nine college students rated these instructors on attributes such as confidence, enthusiasm, optimism, likability and warmth on a scale from one to nine. There was a high degree of consistency between the student's ratings, even though they only had thirty seconds of non-verbal behavior to go on.

At the end of the semester the instructor's actual students rated them on these same attributes. The evaluations of the two groups were significantly correlated on nine of the fifteen measures.[3]

---

[3] The following nine traits were highly correlated: Optimistic .84, Confident .82, Dominant .79, Active .77, Enthusiastic .76, Likable .73, Warm .67, Competent .56, Supportive .55. The other six traits were less so: (Not) anxious .26, Honest .32, Empathetic .45, Attentive .48,

Wow! Thirty seconds of non-verbal behavior produced assessments that were similar to a semester's worth of in-class evaluation. This indicates we have a sophisticated evaluation capability based on the observation of a small amount of non-verbal behavior. And that amount of non-verbal behavior was about to shrink.

Next, they had a student, who was unfamiliar with the study, randomly pick five-second and two-second clips from the original ten-second clips. They picked a new group to rate the teachers based on these shorter clips. The correlation between the end-of-semester evaluations and the five-second and two-second clips was not as high as the ten-second clips, but there was still a high degree of correlation.[4]

People who observed just three, two-second video-clips of non-verbal behavior were able to accurately evaluate another person's confidence, dominance, warmth and likability! This suggests our non-verbal map of the world is vast and capable of immediately generating assessments of others. These assessments, or intuitions, are automatic—remember the angry face—and they influence the decisions of the conscious mind.

Mindsets are inevitable, influential, and they form in seconds. After the first few seconds the interviewer begins to see what they expect to see, and the interview is likely over in a minute or less. But the conscious mind does not yet know this, and the interview continues for forty minutes or more. During the interview, from beginning to end, the "adaptive unconscious [is playing] a major role in selecting, interpreting, and evaluating incoming information."[5] Such is the nature of the cognitive unconscious, and mindsets are a part of this filtering process.

Accepting .50, Professional .53. As can be seen, four of the six traits that failed to make the statistical cut were still within ten points of the "Supportive" trait that did.
[4] This research appeared in: *Ambady, N., & Rosenthal, R. (1993). Half a minute: Predicting teacher evaluations from thin slices of nonverbal behavior and physical attractiveness. Journal of Personality and Social Psychology, 64(3), 431-441.*
[5] Timothy D. Wilson, p. 39.

We are often unaware of all of the fast assessments of non-verbal behavior that are made by the cognitive unconscious. But we don't need to be aware of them for this to affect our conscious decisions, or those of hiring authorities. We saw this happening with the words that flashed on a screen, when non-conscious words influenced conscious thought.

At the end of an interview hiring authorities sometimes struggle to provide reasons why they did not hire a promising candidate. They usually default to something like, "Oh, he was a poor fit." One of the reasons why they struggle may be because their decision was heavily influenced by suggestions from the cognitive unconscious, and they have no direct access to this powerful subconscious mind. No one does. In other words, the interviewer's decision is partly the result of subconscious processes of which he is unaware.

We will spend a good deal of time going over what you say, but for the moment our focus will be on the powerful, mindset-forming speech of non-verbal behavior. Within seconds the cognitive unconscious is using these cues to form accurate evaluations of the person they are watching, and it steers the conscious mind toward hiring those who communicate the most positive and powerful non-verbal message. It is an emotional language that generates feelings—good or bad—that can lead to a jobseeker being hired or rejected.

THE MIRROR NEURON SYSTEM

Researchers at the University of Parma, in Italy, isolated a macaque's neuron that fired whenever they were given a peanut. Put a peanut in the macaque's hand and the neuron activated. But then they noticed something strange. It also activated when the peanut was in the hand of the researcher. They isolated another neuron that fired when the macaque had a peanut in its mouth. That neuron responded the same way when a researcher placed the peanut in their mouth. These observations led to the discovery of the mirror neuron system (MNS).[6]

---

[6] This finding first appeared in a 1992 paper in *Experimental Brain*

Dr. Louann Brizendine wrote the following about the MNS: "The 'I feel what you feel' emotional empathy system. Gets in sync with others' emotions by reading *facial expressions* and interpreting *tone of voice* and other *non-verbal emotional cues*."[7]

Note the emphasis on non-verbal emotional cues. Psychologically healthy human beings feel what others feel based on what they see and hear. When we are in the presence of a sad person, he does not have to say a word and we feel sad. His downcast appearance and facial expression convey a sadness that we experience to a lesser, but undeniable degree. Conversely, when a happy, positive person enters a room we feel his optimism and energy. His smile makes us smile.

We are like emotional tuning forks. Bring a certain emotional vibration into our vicinity and we begin to vibrate and generate the same note.

The MNS helps explain the influence of non-verbal behaviors, their power to shape our evaluations, and their ability to generate emotions that lead some jobseekers to rejections and others to job offers. We see the power of non-verbals in the following story.

NON-VERBAL BEHAVIOR AND PERCEPTION

Neil Rackham and Richard Ruff interviewed a salesperson named David who said the following:

> I joined this corporation because it pays me best. ...I don't believe in its products—they are overpriced and have no better features than the competition. I'm not interested in customers. As far as I'm concerned, I'm in this job for two years. I'm going to make a killing and move on. When I look at a customer I don't see a face, I just see my commission paycheck. I'm prepared to do or say anything which will get some fool to sign money into my pocket.[8]

Research (Vol. 91, No. 1, pages 176-180).
[7] Louann Brizendine, M.D., *The Male Brain* (New York: Harmony Books, 2010), p. xvi. Emphasis mine. She also wrote *The Female Brain*.
[8] Neil Rackham, Richard Ruff, *Managing Major Sales: Practical*

People like David are creepy. They have a psychopath's absence of empathy. From a character standpoint, David was the exact opposite of Alan, his colleague, who said:

> I really believe in this company and its products... and I think we try to achieve the best for our customers. In the eight years I've been in this job, the client has always come first, and I believe that sales success depends on a real and genuine desire to help each customer.[9]

The researchers then asked their customers if they viewed their salesperson to be sincere or insincere? If they were to base their answer on the *substance* of these two individuals, Alan was clearly more sincere than David. However, no one can look inside the human heart. Therefore, these customers based their answers on information that was accessible, namely, non-verbal behavior:

> David was a master of the firm handshake, steady eye contact, a relaxed open posture, the concerned smile and reassuring words. All of these things were behaviors—the customer could see them and be influenced by them. Alan, on the other hand, tended to avoid eye contact. He would sit hunched up, he would be jerky in his speech, and he would say things like, "I can't really answer you." In short his behaviors gave the impression he was concealing something—so customers judged him insincere. The conclusions are simple. Customers judge by what they can see.[10]

David's non-verbal behaviors generated the perception that he was trustworthy while Alan's did the opposite. Alan's words weren't the issue. Yes, he said, "I can't really answer you," and his customers viewed this negatively. However, I can't tell you how many times I've said the exact same thing to customers and it was viewed as a positive. The difference was Alan's non-verbal behaviors and mine. I was looking them straight in the eye, and

---

Strategies for Improving Sales Effectiveness (New York: Harper Business, 1991), pp. 96-97.
[9] Neil Rackham, Richard Ruff, p. 97.
[10] Neil Rackham, Richard Ruff, p. 97.

was confidently standing tall. To my customers it was viewed as an expression of honesty.

It was not Alan's verbal behavior that formed a negative mindset of him in his customer's minds. It was how he expressed his words. His communication style was more powerful than the substance of who he was and what he was saying.

WHEN VERBALS AND NON-VERBALS DISAGREE

In the illustration at the start of this chapter, Bill was nervous as he headed into his job interview. He was stressed to the point where he looked like a dead man walking. Unfortunately, this led to a conflict between his verbal and non-verbal communication. His words were attempting to express one thing (confidence and competence), while his non-verbal expressions said another (I'm scared and lack confidence).

During important, emotionally charged communications, like job interviews, we tend to believe what the non-verbal behaviors are saying more than the words. So, when the words and non-verbal behaviors don't match, the words are casualties in this conflict.

Albert Mehrabian drew this conclusion from his research in 1967 that appeared in a paper entitled, "Decoding of Inconsistent Communications." His study found tone of voice and facial expressions were more influential than words when communicating one's feelings or attitudes.

He later claimed the actual meaning of words was only 7% of the message when communicating one's feelings or attitudes. Meanwhile, tone and body language (including facial expressions), had a respective weighting of 38% and 55%.

Whether his ratios are accurate, or not, is unimportant. What is important is this: In high-risk, high-reward—emotional—situations, non-verbal behaviors are more influential than the words themselves, particularly when the two don't match.

I sometimes demonstrate this to an audience by looking down at the ground, shuffling my feet, adopting a stooped posture and saying in a high-pitched, nasally voice, "I am a powerful leader."

Then I ask, "Would anyone, meeting me for the first time, believe what I am saying?" About the only response I get is laughter.

NON-VERBAL CONTROL

When you are deliriously happy do you have to remind yourself to smile? Do you need to consciously think, "My eyes are sad right now, and yet I am happy. I need to adjust the way my eyes look"?

No conscious thought is necessary, because non-verbal behaviors are a subconscious expression of our emotional state. When we are sad we appear to be sad automatically and, because of the MNS, those around us pick up on these non-verbal cues and feel sad too.

Non-verbal behaviors are subconscious, but we can control them through conscious effort for short periods of time. If someone sees you slouching and says, "You should stand up straight," you can take conscious control of this part of your body language and stand up straight.

However, it is virtually impossible to control our non-verbal behaviors consciously for extended periods of time. This is because our conscious, rational mind does not have the bandwidth to receive a message from the interviewer, decode it, determine how best to respond, encode a message, deliver it to the interviewer, while also focusing on facial expressions, body language and tone of voice. The rational mind's processing speed of forty bits per second is not up to the task.

You may have started an interview thinking, "I'm going to have a warm, relaxed facial expression, and a charming, confident tone," but, unless you are a highly-skilled actor, it is difficult to fake these feelings and stay "in character" for very long. On top of that, these thoughts are easily forgotten during the tense question-and-answer of an interview. Then, absent conscious control, our faked non-verbal behaviors revert to subconsciously expressing our emotional state. And if we are nervous, then our anxiety is clearly written across our face, our tense body language, and our tone, and the interviewer automatically feels what we are feeling.

THE KEY TO CONTROL

Since non-verbal behaviors are subconscious expressions of our emotional state, then how can we control them?

There is only one sure way, and that is by controlling our emotional state.

Great! But how do we do that? How do we control the anxiety that is understandably present during an interview? In the next chapter we will learn how to do this in surprising ways.

6

Mastering Non-Verbal Communication

EMOTIONALLY AND MENTALLY OPTIMAL

There are 11,000,000 bits of information streaming into our minds every second and we consciously use forty of them. The same holds true for the person interviewing you. We tend to focus on the forty-bit part by feeding the interviewer's slow, rational mind a boring diet of data. But what happens when we take advantage of 10,999,960 non-rational, non-conscious bits?

By controlling non-verbal behaviors, our visible expressions of confidence will influence those 10,000,000 visual bits of information flowing into the minds of interviewers every second. Since non-verbal behaviors are subconscious expressions of our emotional state, we gain control over them by controlling our emotional state.

So how do we control our emotional state? By controlling our brain chemistry. We will look at three techniques that achieve this end. Additionally, we will study four more techniques that use our minds to make our emotional state as positive and confident as possible.

These changes in brain chemistry also affect our ability to think, to use those higher mental processes that enable us to solve complex problems, be creative, and so on. Being mentally quick on your feet is critical during job interviews, but unfortunately we are often the opposite, and this is also due to brain chemistry.

THE MIND-BODY CONNECTION

One of the ways we can generate these changes in our brain chemistry is by changing our body posture. Amy Cuddy, a Social Psychologist and an Assistant Professor at the Harvard Business School, took a saliva sample of the men and women who were participating in her study.[1] This gave her a baseline reading of their testosterone level (a hormone associated with dominance and that is secreted less when we are stressed), and cortisol level (a glucocorticoid that is secreted in larger amounts when we are stressed).[2]

Next, the experimental subjects either assumed a high-power pose or a low-power pose for two minutes. There were several high-power poses used in the study but the one I use, and teach others to use, is called the Superman, or Wonder Woman, pose. It is standing up straight, legs slightly apart, with your hands on your hips and the elbows pointing out. High-power poses tend to occupy space.

The low-power poses tend to occupy as little space as possible. The arms remain close to the body. It is more fetal position than Superman, the body language of a person who seems to want to disappear.

Then after assuming either pose for two minutes another saliva sample was obtained and the two samples were compared.

The results were remarkable. The high-power pose increased

---

[1] I highly recommend you view her 2012 TED talk. The link is http://www.ted.com/talks/amy_cuddy_your_body_language_shapes_who _you_are. Or simply google "Amy Cuddy 2012 TED Talk." It is only twenty-one minutes long, is packed with interesting information and has been viewed over 24,000,000 times.

[2] Yes, a woman's ovaries do produce testosterone and the amount in their bloodstream can change hourly.

testosterone levels by 20% while the low-power pose decreased it by 10%. That is a whopping 30% difference in the changes between the two groups. But the effect on cortisol was even more dramatic. The high-power pose reduced it by 25%, while the low-power pose increased it by 15%. The importance of this 40% difference in cortisol levels will become clearer once we look at stress and its impact on the mind and body.

MS. CUDDY STUDIES THE JOB INTERVIEW

These findings were interesting, but fortunately for jobseekers, Ms. Cuddy then tested the impact of these poses on a stressful interaction: the job interview.

There were two groups of people who were both videotaped. One group performed the high-power pose and the other the low-power pose, for two minutes, before their interview. The interviewer was trained to conduct the five-minute interview with a stone-face, showing no emotion, to increase the interviewee's stress level. Evidently, our inability to elicit human emotions from someone during face-to-face talk tends to freak us out.

Finally, coders, who were blind to the hypothesis of the study, viewed the videotapes and graded the performance of both posing groups. The result? They wanted to hire the high-power posers, and the reason was not based on their verbal performance. The coders gave similar grades on the verbal behaviors to both groups. What the interviewee's said during their interviews was similar, but how they said it is what made the difference.

The high-power posers seemed to express more confidence, passion and presence. Their facial expression, tone of voice and body language communicated this, and the coders felt the confidence that the interviewees were feeling. They couldn't help but feel this. It's part of the package of being human.

THE CASE OF BARBARA

I will now share the experience of another one of my clients, Barbara, who came to see me the day before a job interview. She was very anxious, over fifty years old, and did not want to blow this opportunity since there were not a lot of them coming her way. Her nervousness did what it tends to do. It robbed her of any natural charisma she might have possessed. Instead, of appearing as a dynamic solution to a hiring authority's problems she looked like a kind, retiring sort, a person you might want to hug but not necessarily hire.

I had only forty minutes to spend with her, so I focused on ways to help her positively change her emotional state and, therefore, her non-verbal behaviors. I told her about the high-power pose and how she should arrive early to the interview, find a bathroom and stand tall in her stall like Wonder Woman. I also told her to exercise the morning of the interview for reasons that will become clear in the next chapter.

Here is what she wrote to me a few days after the interview:

> Hi Tom,
>
> Sorry for my delay in getting back to you, my life has gotten so busy! I need to let you know that meeting with you was so constructive. I went straight home and studied. Before the interview I set my phone to 2 minutes and did a power pose in the bathroom. I also made sure to exercise in the morning. I walked on the treadmill while memorizing my value statement. At the interview, I didn't even get to say my value statement, they asked me questions right off the bat and asked me to reply with a story. Bingo! I had stories, thanks to you and CTC [Career Transitions Center of Chicago—my note].

Barbara was pursuing a position with a company that worked with Obamacare, getting people signed up, and so on. When I think of anything that is government related, Republican or Democrat, I think, "Bureaucracy. Slow service. No service."

So how long do you think this organization took to get back in touch with her about the results of the interview?

I've asked others and I've gotten answers ranging from two to six weeks. What's your guess?

Here is what Barbara wrote me:

> I can't thank you enough for your help, I felt great and confident going into the interview and they called to give me the job 2 hours later!
>
> I appreciate that you donate your time so a woman like me can find the confidence to succeed in these situations life puts in front of me. My family is so proud of me!
>
> Thanks a million!
>
> Barbara

Now what does that tell you?

Barbara made them *want* her by utilizing the mind-body connection to change her brain chemistry, which changed her emotional state, which changed her non-verbal behaviors. She worked with human nature to generate positive feelings that were non-verbally expressed and felt by the interviewers. The difficult path of job search has now equipped her with tools that can favorably impact the rest of her life. Whenever she needs to be more influential during an important meeting she can use these tools prior to the meeting to become so.

When we communicate, and our verbal and non-verbal behaviors are in synch, we have an authentic voice that gets job offers. An ambiguous voice—when our words say one thing and our non-verbal behaviors say another—receives the silent treatment. An authentic voice can create a great first impression and the rest of the interview can build upon this solid foundation. The hiring authority's cognitive unconscious will begin generating an emotionally powerful message, "Barbara's the one! Hire her! Now!" And the hiring authority responds to these suggestions that force their way into consciousness in ways we are only beginning to understand.

THE CHASE IS ON

Stress negatively affects our brain chemistry and our ability to think. When our understanding is illuminated on this point we are more likely to do whatever it takes to reduce the impact of stress. The following fantastic experience will help illustrate stress's impact.

I was walking down Michigan Avenue, in the beautiful city of Chicago, past the Art Institute, when one of its iconic lions came to life. The lion roared, looked at me, and looked hungry. I did not even think about what I should do. Logical thought processing would take too much time, so a more primitive part of my brain took over, initiating a cascade of mind-body changes to keep me alive:

> The overarching principle of the fight-or-flight response is marshaling resources for immediate needs in lieu of building for the future—act now, ask questions later. The hormonal rush of epinephrine focuses the body, increasing heart rate and blood pressure and dilating the bronchial tubes of the lungs to carry more oxygen to the muscles. ...In this scenario the biological imperatives like eating and reproduction are put on the backburner. The digestive system shuts down; the muscles used to contract the bladder relax so as to not lose glucose; and saliva stops flowing.[3]

With that last bit of data we start to recognize the all-too-familiar stress response that can be caused by lions, or job interviews: cotton mouth. The stress hormone, cortisol, spikes and testosterone levels go down as "biological imperatives like ... reproduction are put on the backburner." Some of these same changes occur when we adopt a low-power pose.

As the authors continue, they use the example of public speaking causing this stress response, but we could just as easily replace this with the stress caused by job interviewing. They write:

> If you've ever faced a nerve wracking public-speaking situation, you've experienced this shift in the form of a racing heart and cotton mouth. *Your muscles and your*

---

[3] John J. Ratey, MD, Eric Hagerman, *Spark: The Revolutionary New Science of Exercise and the Brain* (New York: Little, Brown and Company, 2008), pp. 63-64. I highly recommend this book. It is well written and full of valuable and interesting information, and it will play a central role in the next two chapters.

> *brain get stiff, and you lose all hope of being flexible and engaging.* ...None of this is particularly helpful when you're up at the podium, but the body responds in essentially the same way whether you're staring down a hungry lion or a restless audience.[4]

In essence, my normal functions are put on hold for the sake of channeling all that I have to those parts of my body that are essential to survival. That's great news for those odd days when I am being chased by a lion down Michigan Avenue, but it is bad news when I am interviewing for a job, because it affects my ability to think:

> The pre-frontal cortex (PFC)—the most evolved brain region—subserves our highest-order cognitive abilities. However, it is also the brain region that is the most sensitive to the detrimental affects of stress exposure. Even quite mild acute uncontrollable stress can cause a rapid and dramatic loss of pre-frontal cognitive abilities.[5]

It is difficult to communicate effectively when our IQ operates at the level of a rhesus monkey. Therefore, mitigating the effects of the stress-response is critical to job search success, and the way the high-power pose does this is by reducing cortisol and increasing testosterone.

Epinephrine is the fast-acting agent of the stress response. It enters the blood stream quickly and leaves it quickly. Not so with cortisol. It can take hours for it to leave our system. Yet a simple high-power pose reduced the level of cortisol by twenty-five percent in just two minutes. That is impressive.

One of the illustrations Ms. Cuddy uses for low cortisol and high testosterone is an alpha-male ape. These leaders of the pack tend to have a relatively higher testosterone and lower cortisol level than the other apes in their shrewdness.[6] Meanwhile, those at the bottom

---

[4] Ratey, Hagerman, p. 64. My emphasis.
[5] Amy F. T. Arnsten, "Stress Signaling pathways that impair prefrontal cortex structure and function: Nat. Rev. Neurosci. 2009 Jun: 10(6): 410-422.
[6] A group of apes is called a shrewdness of apes and a group of crows is

of the dominance hierarchy are seriously stressed out:

> Establish male monkeys in a social group, and over the course of days to months they'll figure out where they stand with respect to one another. Once a stable dominance hierarchy has emerged, the last place you want to be is on the bottom.... Such subordinate males show a lot of the physiological indices of chronically turning on their stress responses. And often these animals wind up with atherosclerotic plaques—their arteries are all clogged up.[7]

The same thing happens to female apes. The ones "stuck in subordinate positions have twice the atherosclerosis as dominant females, even when on a low-fat diet."[8] Ms. Cuddy's research on power dynamics also seems to be related to stress reduction, and creating a positive, confident emotional state.

We can also create this positive emotional state by using our minds.

WHO WAS CONSTANTIN STANISLASKY?

Constantin Stanislavsky was the administrator of the Moscow Art Theater and is credited with the creation of method acting. It is a technique that attempts to change an actor's emotional state so that their non-verbal behaviors convey the emotions the script requires.

Jobseekers face the same problem confronting actors. They need to speak authentically. The job interviewing script requires an emotional state that is infectiously confident and positive. Just as the method acting technique helps actors change their emotional state, it can also help jobseekers do the same.

Does it work? Yes, but of the seven techniques I teach people so that they can change their emotional state, this is often the one they neglect. That is unfortunate, because it is also one of the most

---

called a murder of crows. Whoever dreamed up these designations had a good sense of humor.
[7] Robert M. Sapolsky, *Why Zebras Don't Get Ulcers* (New York: Henry Holt and Company, 2004), p. 44.
[8] Sapolsky, p. 52.

powerful ways of controlling nervousness while waiting in the lobby for your first interview.

UTILIZING THE METHOD

There are variations of this technique, but I use the following approach. I recall memories of joyous achievements. One of them was graduating from the U.S. Army's Ranger School and ending its 58 days of psychological and physical abuse.[9] (Since we volunteered for this treatment, one cannot fault the U.S. Army.)

When it was over I felt a great sense of relief and pride at having passed this test. In my mind I see myself smiling. I feel the Ranger Instructor pinning the Ranger tab on my shoulder. I hear him say, "Congratulations Ranger Payne." I see the red clay ground and the pine trees at Fort Benning, Georgia, and I smell the pine trees as well. The sensory details are important. They help make the emotional recollection visceral.

When I do this I generate a feeling of elation, a sense of confidence that is willing to take on any obstacle, and the emotional state is real. Then I add this important detail: I say to myself a phrase that I associate with this memory. My phrase is, "I did it! And I can do it again and again and again." Then, after having recalled this memory many times, and associating it with this phrase, I can now recall the emotion by simply saying the phrase.

How do I use it? Before I speak in public, I will go to a restroom—if no other room is available—stand tall in my stall in my Superman pose, recall my Ranger School graduation and say to myself, "I did it! And I can do it again and again and again."

My non-verbal behaviors will now express my confident, emotional state. My arms will move freely from the shoulder. I will not have the penguin arms of fear, the ones where the upper arms seem glued to the body while the lower arms make weak movements. My tone will be authoritative. There will be a passionate sound of conviction in my voice that will be both heard

---

[9] Ranger School has since gotten longer. It used to consist of three phases: city, mountain and swamp. Now it also has a desert phase.

and felt by my audience, and this same influential, powerful voice can be yours during job interviews if you practice these exercises.

YOUR TURN

Your experience might be much more significant than mine, or much less. It doesn't matter, because we are not competing with one another. What does matter is that the experience you recall is emotionally significant to you.

The emotion you want to generate is the feeling of achievement and triumph. If you have ever won something, and it brought you feelings of elation and mastery, then this experience is a good one for you to recall. Perhaps a boss, who was important to you, praised you for something, in front of your peers, and the confidence this gave you marked the point where your career took off. It might be graduating from high school or college. It could be winning an athletic endeavor, or scoring a personal best record in a 5K, or a marathon.

Whatever it is, try to recall the feeling and the associated sensory images. Smells are particularly potent when it comes to remembering events and the emotions associated with them, but sight and sound are a must.

Next, develop a phrase that works for you, and associate it with this memory. You are welcome to use mine, and several attendees of my seminars have done so.

Then rehearse it. Rehearse it every morning before you start your job-search related tasks. It will help you deal with stress, ensure you have a positive attitude as you start your day, and it will become easier to do after each session. Then, when the job interview arrives, you will be ready to benefit from its maximum impact.

THE HIGH-POWER POSE THAT FAILED

Maybe it was the bright lights, or the tripod-mounted, high-definition video camera, but whatever it was, my client looked nervous during his mock interview. He had just finished his high-power pose and his non-verbal behaviors were still betraying him. So was his brain's capacity to operate at a high level. He could not remember his script, and his answer to the "tell me about yourself" question amounted to a laundry list of details that failed to illustrate his value in any way. It was not the branding statement we had created together.

What happened?

He was a bit of hard case, an acid test for any technique. He came to me admitting how he struggled to express himself with confidence. I remember our first meeting. As we talked he was unaware that his hand stroked the top of his thigh, unconsciously communicating his anxiety. And this wasn't a job interview; we were simply getting to know one another. His deep-seated insecurity about his poor communication abilities, and having them captured on tape, triggered a stress response that overwhelmed everything else.

His biggest problem seemed to be his breathing. It was shallow and, as a result, his voice had a higher pitch. His words did not have enough air to generate the sonorous under-tones that make a speaking voice both pleasant and powerful. As it turns out, Ms. Cuddy's high-power pose does not work very well unless you breathe. Then again, neither does anything else, except for what I taught him: breathing exercises.

We made the following adjustment before the second mock interview. I had him take three, slow, deep breaths following this method. I took a deep breath and showed him how it distended my belly. Then, on top of this deep breath, I inhaled again. My belly distended a little more. Then I inhaled a third time and very little extra air came in. Following this, I exhaled slowly. He then took three deep breaths—inhaling three times with each breath—and we then went into our second mock interview.

The difference was immediately noticeable. He was much more relaxed, his tone was deeper and more authoritative. His answers showed he was thinking clearly, as he easily recited his prepared answers to typical interviewing questions.

I shared this story with Ms. Cuddy and she replied:

> Yes, deep breathing seems to be one of the important mechanisms driving the effect. And deep breathing has been studied: it decreases cortisol and also affects the vagus nerve, decreasing the parasympathetic nervous system's fight or flight response.

In other words, it is another tool to use to reverse the damaging impact of stress.

BEFORE THE INTERVIEW

I highly recommend the following schedule before an interview. Exercise vigorously a few hours before the interview so that you can shower, or go on a vigorous walk closer to the time of the interview, but not to the point of sweating. (More on this in the next chapter.) Do the high-power pose combined with the method acting exercise about ten minutes before the interview. Then, while you are sitting in the lobby waiting, take the occasional deep breath and exhale slowly. At the same time recall your method-acting phrase—"I did it! And I can do it again and again and again." This will have positive effects on your brain chemistry and minimize the effects of stress, ensuring that the real, confident, competent you, is the one who shows up for the interview.

FINAL THOUGHTS

I've interviewed many people and I've felt their anxiety and nervousness. But I've also felt a talented jobseeker's beaming confidence.

I still remember one interview that I conducted fourteen years ago. He was a short man whose hair had gone completely white. He was about fifty-five years old, slightly overweight, a good bit older than most of my other Region Managers, but he had a broad smile and a look of supreme confidence.

I mention him to jobseekers who may be older and are concerned about their marketability. I tell them, "After the first few minutes I did not recognize his height, lined face or hair color. I just thought, 'This guy is as polished as anyone I've ever met. I'll bet his customers will love him.' " And they did after he joined our team.

Mastering the subconscious speech of non-verbal behavior is one of the most important job search tasks. It affects our ability to communicate, influence others, and interview well. Those who master this form of speech will connect powerfully with hiring authorities, and will benefit from these skills for the rest of their life. The three techniques I've just described, and the fourth and fifth ones that appear in the next two chapters, will set you well on your way toward communicating with authority. The sixth and seventh techniques will appear in the chapters *Networking Through Informational Interviewing* and *The H.E.A.R.T Principles*.

7

Run For Your Life

THE MIND-BODY CONNECTION REVISITED

There is another way to take control of our brain's chemistry and leverage this mind-body connection, and I believe it is even more powerful than the high-power pose, deep breathing and method acting. It is rarely considered by the jobseekers I meet, but the research supporting its ability to favorably alter our brain chemistry, and our emotional state, is growing every year. For some this will be good news, for others…uh, more challenging.

One of the best ways to favorably change our brain chemistry is through exercise. Exercise affects neurotransmitters and growth factors, and these changes can affect our mood, perception, thinking ability, motivation, in sum, virtually everything required for job search success.

NEUROTRANSMITTERS

Neurotransmitters are chemicals that brain cells, or neurons, release to enable the transmission of an impulse from one neuron to another. They enable neurons to communicate and each neurotransmitter has different functions. The three we will concentrate on are serotonin, dopamine and norepinephrine, because most "…of the drugs we use to improve mental health target one or more of these three neurotransmitters."[1]

For example, the anti-anxiety and anti-depression drug, Prozac, targets serotonin. Serotonin influences mood, impulsivity and acts like the policeman of the brain, because it helps control brain activity. Dopamine is the neurotransmitter targeted by the drug Ritalin that is prescribed to treat attention-deficit/hyperactivity disorder, or ADHD. Dopamine is involved with reward, learning and attention. And norepinephrine "often amplifies signals that influence attention, perception, motivation and arousal."[2]

Keeping our neurotransmitters properly regulated is essential, because of their impact on such a wide spectrum of emotional and mental states, and we can regulate them through exercise:

> …I tell people that going for a run is like taking a little bit of Prozac and a little bit of Ritalin because, like the drugs, exercise elevates these neurotransmitters. It's a handy metaphor to get the point across, but the deeper explanation is that *exercise balances neurotransmitters —along with the rest of the neurochemicals in the brain*. And as you'll see, keeping your brain in balance can change your life.[3]

ANXIETY

In the early stages of job search it can be a struggle to gain control over our fears, for it is human to feel anxious while struggling to find work. Unfortunately, when we are anxious we communicate this to others in subtle, non-verbal ways. Exercise helps us overcome our anxiety:

> …the majority of studies show that aerobic exercise significantly alleviates symptoms of any anxiety disorder. But exercise also helps the average person reduce normal

---

[1] Ratey, Hagerman, p. 37.
[2] Ratey, Hagerman, p. 37.
[3] Ratey, Hagerman, p. 37, my emphasis.

feelings of anxiousness.[4]

I don't believe I've ever worked with a job search client who had an extreme anxiety disorder, like agoraphobia, the fear of open or enclosed public spaces, and particularly crowded ones. Yet exercise proved as effective as drugs in treating agoraphobia in a randomized, placebo-controlled trial conducted by Dr. Andreas Broocks in 1997.

There were three groups—exercise, drug and placebo—and the exercise group did not start producing positive results, equal to the drug group, until the tenth week. The delay was largely due to their being unable to run outside until week six.

Could Dr. Broocks have chosen a more challenging disorder to benefit from running outside? Perhaps, but it is a dramatic example of the benefits generated by exercise.

DEPRESSION

The connection between exercise and treating depression is a strong one. "In fact, it is largely through depression research that we know as much as we do about what exercise does for the brain. It counteracts depression at almost every level.

"In Britain, doctors now use exercise as a first-line treatment for depression...."[5]

How often do you need to exercise to have such a therapeutic impact? Dr. James Blumenthal, at Duke University, ran a study that compared an exercise group, a group that took Zoloft (a Selective Serotonin Reuptake Inhibitor), and a group that took Zoloft and exercised. The exercise group, and the exercise-Zoloft group, either walked or jogged for thirty minutes, three times a week, at between 70-85% of aerobic capacity. This also included a ten-minute warm-up and a five-minute cool down, or forty-five minutes of exercise. Half of each group benefited by experiencing remission, or complete recovery. In other words, exercise performed as well as the drug, and the drug plus exercise, in

---

[4] Ratey, Hagerman, p. 92.
[5] Ratey, Hagerman, p. 114.

treating depression.

One of the most important contributions exercise makes when it comes to our emotional state is the way it reduces stress.

EXERCISE AND STRESS

Aerobic exercise stresses the body, yet the stress response caused by exercise is a healthy one. Not only does it regulate the neurotransmitters, it also produces growth factors that stimulate the creation of new neurons, and new capillaries to deliver an increased amount of energy to the brain. Though the brain only weighs around three pounds, it consumes about 20-30% of the body's oxygen and 70% of its glucose. When you have 100 billion neurons and one quadrillion synaptic connections to feed, many of them generating electrical impulses, a lot of food is necessary.

Most people will readily accept that exercise relieves stress. They've experienced this and don't need to read scientific research confirming this. They also don't need to be told that job search is stressful. They've experienced this as well. But what they may not be aware of is the way stress is damaging their health, the accuracy of their perception, their feelings toward others, and their chances at job search success.

Dr. Robert Sapolsky, a professor of biology, neuroscience, and neurosurgery at Stanford University, wrote the following about exercise and stress reduction:

> Exercise is a great counter to stress for a number of reasons.
>
> ...[E]xercise makes you feel good. ...And most of all, the stress-response is about preparing your body for a sudden explosion of muscular activity. You reduce tension if you actually turn on the stress-response for that purpose instead of merely stewing in the middle of some time-wasting meeting.
>
> Finally, there's some evidence that exercise makes for a

> smaller stress-response to various psychological stressors.[6]

Then after listing its many benefits, he offers some of the following qualifications. The stress-reducing, mood-enhancing effect of exercise lasts for only a few hours to a day. This is an argument for exercising daily, and a few hours before the interview. Another qualification is exercise needs to occur regularly, for a sustained period of time, for us to realize its many benefits, but some benefits occur after one session.

IMPROVED BRAIN FUNCTION

Stress can diminish our ability to think clearly, while exercise can enhance our cognitive powers. What is most encouraging is the way this cognitive gain can occur after just one workout. In the following experiment the workout referred to was one thirty-five-minute session of running on a treadmill that elevated the participant's heart-rate to between sixty and seventy percent of its maximum:

> Half of them [the adults aged 50-64—my note] watched a movie and the other half exercised, and they were tested before the session, immediately after, and again twenty minutes later. The movie watchers showed no change, but the runners improved their processing speed and cognitive flexibility after just one workout. Cognitive flexibility is an important executive function that reflects our ability to shift thinking and to produce a steady flow of creative thoughts and answers as opposed to a regurgitation of the usual responses. The trait correlates with high-performance in intellectually demanding jobs. [For example, the job interview—my note.] So if you have an important brainstorming session scheduled, going for a short intense run during lunchtime is a smart idea.[7]

This is one of the reasons why I asked Barbara to exercise in the morning prior to her interview. This, combined with the high-

---

[6] Sapolsky, p. 401.
[7] Ratey, Hagerman, p. 54.

power pose, elevated her mood and confidence to a point where it made her once tentative, timid voice both captivating and compelling. And it also enabled her cognitive abilities to function at a higher level.

Exercise also "prepares and encourages nerve cells to bind to one another, which is the cellular basis for logging in new information...."[8] In other words, if you need to memorize your branding statement, or stories—and you will, if you want to separate yourself from the interviewing pack—then exercise will help you do this. I highly recommend exercising before rehearsing, interviewing or tackling a difficult problem.

NEUROGENESIS

Exercise not only affects neurotransmitters, it also spurs the growth of new brain cells, or neurons. This is called neurogenesis, and until the 1990s most scientists believed our brains had a fixed number of neurons that declined as we aged. But the reality is we can generate new neurons through exercise.

There is a family of proteins called "factors," and they help build the circuitry of our brain. Brain-derived neurotrophic factor (BDNF) is like fertilizer in that it causes the cellular growth associated with learning to occur. Dr. Carl Cotman, director of the Institute for Brain Aging and Dementia, University of California, Irvine, first noted how its production was stimulated by exercise.

After conducting a long-term study into cognitive decline, he found three variables that were shared by those who suffered the least amount of decline: education, self-sufficiency and exercise. The first two variables made intuitive sense, but why was exercise seemingly linked to brain health?

Cotman devised an exercise program for mice—animals that love to exercise—and it had them running a couple of kilometers on a running wheel for either two, four or seven nights a week. The control group had no access to the running wheel.

---

[8] Ratey, Hagerman, p. 53.

He then injected them with a molecule that binds to BDNF and discovered that the farther the mice ran the more BDNF production occurred. But what surprised him was the growth of new neurons in the hippocampus, the brain structure associated with memory and ravaged by Alzheimer's. Why would exercise make neurons grow there? Why not in the areas of the brain associated with physical movement like the somatosensory cortex? He repeated his experiment to make sure he wasn't mistaken, because he was so surprised by this finding. The second experiment produced the same result.

Exercise, by itself, is not enough to grow and sustain new neurons. Mental activity is a critical part of the process, because for new neurons to survive they need to be put to work. As we move into the verbal realm there will be plenty of mental work to do.

WHAT'S THE DOSE?

Hopefully you have been sold on the benefits of exercise and the way it can not only help you improve your emotional state and cognitive capabilities, but can also help you maintain a higher level of functioning later on in life. The question now becomes, "How much exercise?" In the next chapter I will try and answer this question, and also show how the varying intensity levels produce different benefits.

8

Survival of the Fit

EXERCISE PROGRAM

You don't need to adopt the training program of an Ironman competitor for exercise to produce great results. However, different intensity levels produce different results, and this may lead you to intensify your exercise routine.

As several studies noted, exercise is good, but more exercise is better. The *Spark* program recommends working out six days a week with two of the workouts being intense and shorter in duration. The intensity is measured by one's heart rate, and the two intense sessions elevate it to 75%-90% of one's maximum heart rate (MHR) for about forty-five minutes. The other four sessions are longer and moderately intense (65%-75% of MHR for about one hour). However, as the authors stress, it takes time to progress to an intense exercising level, and this important topic will be covered toward the end of the chapter.

I follow a slightly different routine. I run five times a week, with three runs being longer (four to six miles), and that operate in the "intense" exercise zone. And two shorter runs (three miles), operating in the "moderate" intensity zone, followed by weight lifting.

Each of the five runs begins with a warm-up, and three of them end with at least three three-minute sprints followed by a cool down for reasons to be noted later.

THREE TYPES OF WORK OUTS

The three types of workout are:

1. Mild: Some form of exercise like walking that gets your heart to beat at 55%-65% of your MHR.
2. Moderate: Some form of exercise like jogging (65%-75% of MHR).
3. Intense: Some form of exercise like running (75%-90% of MHR).

CALCULATING YOUR MAXIMUM HEART RATE

Your maximum heart rate is 220 minus your age. This number is then multiplied by an intensity percentage. Let's say you are 40 years old and you want to work out at a high-intensity level (90%). Then your MHR during exercise would be 162: (220 – 40 = 180 MHR) (180 X .9 = 162).

The following schedule simplifies the math:

Percentage of Maximum Heart Rate (MHR) And Beats Per Minute (BPM)				
Age	55% MHR	65%	75%	90%
20	110 BPM	130	150	180
30	105	124	143	171
40	**99**	**117**	**135**	**162**
50	94	111	128	153
60	88	104	120	144
70	83	98	113	135

Here is how to read this chart. If you are 40 years old, then 55% of your MHR is 99 beats per minute (BPM), 65% of your MHR is 117 BPM, 75% is 135 BPM, and your ceiling is 90% of your MHR, or 162 BPM. Above this level you should not go.

The important thing is to exercise in ways that you enjoy. Pilates? Great! Yoga? Why not! Swimming? Perfect! Just wear a heart-rate monitor, if possible, because how hard you work out will determine the benefits you will receive.

MILD WORK OUT BENEFITS: 55%-65% MHR

Walking is a mild work out that still produces tremendous health benefits. It releases free-tryptophan into the blood stream, which is behind the production of serotonin, the mood stabilizer. It also increases the production of dopamine and norepinephrine.

Why did the body develop this response to the increased effort of walking? Some hypothesize that these brain benefits were required for our ancestors to be successful hunters. They had to doggedly pursue their prey over long distances:

> When you look at this in the evolutionary context of Heinrich's endurance predator, it makes elegant sense: while tracking their prey, our ancestors needed to have the patience, optimism, focus and motivation to keep at it. All these traits are influenced by serotonin, dopamine and norepinephrine.[1]

We are not hunting antelope in the wild, but our job search does require "patience, optimism, focus and motivation."

There are added benefits to ratcheting up the intensity of your workouts. So, when you can walk for an hour at a level where it is difficult to carry on a conversation, then you are probably ready to move up to the next level.

MODERATE WORK OUT BENEFITS: 65%-75% MHR

Joggers fall into this category and, according to *Spark's* authors,

---

[1] Ratey, Hagerman, p. 251.

four of your six workouts during the week should be in this moderate range. This stresses the body's need for oxygen and glucose more than walking, and the body responds to this stress by producing growth factors like vascular endothelial growth factor (VEGF) and fibroblast growth factor (FGF-2). Within two hours of being exposed to these factors, cells start dividing to produce new vessels. This occurs in the brain, as does neurogenesis and cell binding.

The body starts to release antioxidants to take care of potentially destructive free radicals and other things that can rupture healthy cells. Yes, aerobic exercise is your personal source of antioxidants.

Your heart muscle also responds by producing atrial natriuretic peptide (ANP). It helps the body manage its response to workout-induced stress by reducing the noise in the brain. When you feel calm at the end of a workout, like your stress has melted away, it is in part due to the increase of ANP.

INTENSE WORK OUT BENEFITS: 75%-90% MHR

This level of effort is perceived as an all-out attack on the body, and its stress response is appropriately powerful. Returning to the hunter image, imagine him approaching his prey. The antelope was not designed to go the long distances this human hunter could go. But the antelope can still generate a few last-second survival bursts. So, for the hunter to catch its prey he must be able to stress his system to its maximum level by sprinting to his target. He arrives at his target exhausted, but he needs to focus on the prey and not his pain. The body responds to this maximum level of effort as follows:

> One of the key differences between moderate and high intensity exercise is that once you get closer to your maximum, and especially when you get into the anaerobic range, the pituitary gland in your brain unleashes human growth hormone (HGH). This is what life-extension groups call the fountain of youth.[2]

---

[2] Ratey, Hagerman, p. 255.

HGH production declines with age. By middle age we are producing one-tenth of what we produced as children. Also blocking production are all of the side effects of a sedentary lifestyle, like excess fatty acids in the bloodstream and insulin resistance. Improving brain health is one of its many benefits: "Researchers believe it can reverse the loss of brain volume that naturally occurs as you age."[3]

The goal for the majority of your workout is aerobic exercise, combined with a few brief excursions into the anaerobic-intensity range. In anaerobic exercise the muscles can't get enough oxygen from the blood stream, so they start to metabolize energy stores that are less efficient. It is tough to say when you cross over into anaerobic exercise, but if you are running at a pace that you can't maintain for forty-five minutes, then you are probably there.

Sprints can briefly put you in this anaerobic zone. I mentioned that I end most of my runs with three three-minute sprints. These sprints are separated by walking .15 miles at a slow, 3 MPH pace, to slow down my heart rate. Here is the reason why I do this:

> ...Normally HGH stays in the bloodstream only a few minutes, but a session of sprinting can keep the level elevated for up to four hours. In the brain HGH balances neurotransmitter levels, and boosts the production of all the growth factors I've mentioned. But it seems to have the most dramatic impact on IGF-1 [Insulin Growth Factor-1—my note.] the evolutionary lynchpin tying together activity, fuel, and learning. It gets into the very cell nucleus and switches on genes that crank up the mechanisms of neuronal growth.[4]

Research shows that adding a few three-minute sprints can produce a significantly higher increase in BDNF than lower intensity exercise. This growth factor has a particularly beneficial effect on neurons. If you sprinkle BDNF on a neuron in a petri dish it will start to sprout new dendritic branches, the very thing occurring

---

[3] Ratey, Hagerman, p. 255.
[4] Ratey, Hagerman, p. 255.

during learning.

Why not add it to the end of every run? Because one of my runs is followed by a heavy dose of weightlifting using my legs (squats, and so on), and I want my legs to be strong before these weight sessions. Squats also have a significant impact on the production of HGH. The other run is an entire session of sprints that is typically called interval training or speed work.

IS IT WORTH IT?

Is slowly climbing the fitness ladder to the point where you can safely do high-intensity intermittent exercise (HIIE) worth it? It all depends on what your goals are. If your goal is to regulate your neurotransmitters and produce a healthier emotional state, then walking will do. But if one of your goals is to get the additional benefits listed above, and get rid of subcutaneous and abdominal body fat, then HIIE may be required.

> The effect of regular aerobic exercise on body fat is negligible; however, other forms of exercise may have a greater impact on body composition. For example, emerging research examining high-intensity intermittent exercise (HIIE) indicates that it may be more effective at reducing subcutaneous and abdominal body fat than other types of exercise. ...Regular HIIE has been shown to significantly increase both aerobic and anaerobic fitness. HIIE also significantly lowers insulin resistance....[5]

If your goal is fat reduction, then running at a moderate pace will not be enough to get you there. You will need to mix in interval training. However, there is a potentially big problem with sprinting and interval work. Unless you have a strong aerobic foundation, it can hurt you more than help you. Even for experienced runners, it is the type of exercise that is most likely to produce injury. I recommend medical advice from your doctor before attempting this for the first time.

---

[5] Boutcher, S. (2011) High intensity intermittent exercise and fat loss. J Obes, v. 2011. doi: 10.1155/2011/868305

Since exercise is about getting healthier, we need to start slowly, and make injury prevention a top goal. Walking is a great way to start, and I recommend wearing a heart-rate monitor to keep track of your heart's response to exercise-stress. It will also help you understand your body's capabilities and safely increase the distance and speed of your walking, jogging and running.

SEE IT, BE IT

We are going to take a break from the racetrack and look at another technique that I use to control my emotional state.

When you are an introvert whose major strengths are in the realm of strategic and analytical thinking—like me—it is easy to appear cold and distant. The mental world of focused thought is not warm and fuzzy; it's glacial. And so, one of the exercises I used to help me project warmth was visualization. I would see myself meeting the interviewer and I would be smiling. In my visualization exercise, this would cause the interviewer to smile.

I would see myself totally relaxed, comfortable in my skin, projecting a relaxed confidence without a trace of arrogance. The interviewer would ask me, "Tell me about yourself," and I would visualize my saying the answer I had scripted and memorized. I would see him ask me the question that was the toughest one I would face. Again, I would smile, and rehearse this answer also. I was not audibly saying a single word, but in my visualization exercise I was.

I would watch the interviewer's body language change as this exercise went on, and both of us laughing at a joke. In short, I was creating a mental program for my mind and body to follow come the day of the interview.

Does visualization help? Many of the world's greatest athletes swear by it, and research backs up its value:

> World Champion Golfer, Jack Nicklaus has said: "I never hit a shot, not even in practice, without having a very sharp in-focus picture of it in my head."

> Brain studies now reveal that thoughts produce the same

mental instructions as actions. Mental imagery impacts many cognitive processes in the brain: motor control, attention, perception, planning, and memory. So the brain is getting trained for actual performance during visualization. It's been found that mental practices can enhance motivation, increase confidence and self-efficacy, improve motor performance, prime your brain for success, and increase states of flow – all relevant to achieving your best life![6]

My experience with visualization is this: Performing it prior to interviewing increased my confidence. It made the stressful interview seem familiar, comfortable and less threatening. It became familiar because this interview had happened many times in my mind. Then, when I met the interviewer during those critical first few minutes, my non-verbal behaviors were warm and confident, just like I visualized them to be. The results? A positive mind-set about me formed quickly. It also resisted change and assimilated all additional information to fit this image. It helped me experience interviewing success against all odds.

If you were to look at my non-verbals prior to these techniques I am sure they would have expressed an intensity that was overwhelming and off-putting. Why? Because I am an intense sort who, when placed in an intense situation, becomes more intense. This was not the path to job search success.

However, visualizing, exercising, and using the other techniques modified my natural tendencies in a positive way.

Realigning job search with human nature requires our developing an understanding of how we tick, what makes us happy or sad, clear-headed or muddled, and hopefully this chapter has helped you progress down this path.

---

[6] https://www.psychologytoday.com/blog/flourish/200912/seeing-is-believing-the-power-visualization. From a post published by A. J. LeVan, December 3, 2009 in *Flourish*. LeVan works at the Clinical Research Unit at the University of Pennsylvania, Abramson Cancer Center.

SUMMARY

You have received five techniques that can turn a nervous, anxious emotional state into its opposite. Before this book is over you will receive two more techniques and they are powerful.

I've personally experienced the power of these techniques and have witnessed the impact they have had on my client's job search. I encourage you to use them on a daily basis until you come to the point where you can create this emotional state by breathing deeply, adjusting your posture, exercising, or simply saying the words, "I did it! And I can do it again and again and again."

Now that we have gained control of the way we non-verbally communicate we can start to work on adjusting the style of our verbal communication. But before we start telling people who we are, we need to find this out.

PART 3:
MASTERING VERBAL COMMUNICATION

9

Self-Discovery

BRANDS

Most jobseekers don't know their own strengths. Until jobseekers understand the potential value they bring to an organization, they can't do a very good job of speaking about it. This makes self-discovery our first step toward mastering verbal communication.

It is not an easy first step to take. Some people struggle with this part of the process for weeks and months. I think I will be able to shorten the time this takes for you, but it will still take time. Perhaps the best way to start this journey is by modifying our self-concept. We are now unique brands, and how this idea applies to us is best illustrated by looking at a well-known brand like Apple.

What do you think of when you think of the Apple brand? Its products are intuitive, or user-friendly. They must conform to a simple design philosophy. For example, Steve Jobs never allowed a second mouse button because he thought it was inelegant. To Apple, design considerations were more important than missing out on some functionality.

These attributes are a distillation of Apple's strengths, or what it does well. If Apple started to produce products that were complex and cluttered, its brand would suffer.

Likewise, when hiring authorities are shopping for new hires they want to understand the nature of the new hire's brand. Namely, what are their distinctive strengths and capabilities? If we can communicate this concisely and clearly, we will have a huge advantage over the majority of our competitors. It will enable us to answer the difficult question,

"TELL ME ABOUT YOURSELF."

Jobseekers struggle with this question like few others. They know it is coming, they write out their answer and rehearse it, and yet their answer falls flat. This question is an invitation to share their brand, their value proposition, but since they don't know what that is, this question is often answered with autobiographical filler: "I worked as a marketing manager at Acme for two years and then was promoted to marketing director. Yadda, yadda, yadda." Or they take the bait and respond to this invitation to sell yourself and boast for three minutes, "I achieved this and this and this, and am number one in this, and great at this, and I've never failed at anything." The answer quickly becomes tiresome and annoying. As you will see, stating what your strengths are doesn't look and feel like this.

STRENGTHS

Marcus Buckingham spent nearly two decades as a researcher at the Gallup organization, a leader in strengths research, and he defines strengths as follows: A strength is "consistent near-perfect performance in an activity."[1]

Strengths are activities we enjoy, things we do because we love doing them. They are intrinsically motivating. Or, as Mr. Buckingham put it, "The acid test of a strength? The ability is a strength only if you can fathom yourself doing it repeatedly, happily, and successfully."[2]

---

[1] Marcus Buckingham, *Now, Discover Your Strengths* (New York: Gallup, Inc., 2001), p. 23.
[2] Buckingham, p. 26.

WEAKNESSES

Strengths are abilities my personality is inclined toward exercising, while I am disinclined toward engaging my weaknesses.

Take a moment to think of something you don't enjoy doing. For me, it is filing. I loathe the mindless monotony of the task, the need to create new folders, everything about it, but I have to do it.

Okay, you've thought about something you hate doing. Now ask yourself, "If I work at it, can I make this a strength?" The answer is, "No!" Can you see yourself doing something you hate to do repeatedly and enjoyably? Are you able to perform this task consistently at a near-perfect level? Not once or twice, but consistently over a period of years.

A weakness can never be a strength. We can operate in non-preferred areas, but we will never excel in these areas, because we don't like working on these tasks. Our hope is to avoid them, but that is not always possible. When circumstances force us to complete these tasks, we can and will do so, but our work is half-hearted and, usually, only the minimum requirements are met.

LEVERAGING STRENGTHS

Successful companies focus on using their strengths. Apple is leveraging its design expertise to enter the new market of wearable tech, namely, watches. Just compare their product to Samsung's, one of their biggest competitors. The difference in their focus on design is obvious.

We also need to leverage our strengths, because our strengths are what we do well. A strengths-focus works with human nature, our unique preferences, how genetics and the environment shaped our development. It will help us on the path to job search success and success in life, because we can then consciously and intentionally leverage them to produce greater results. But until we know our strengths, we are either accidentally using them or failing to use them.

I was on a European consulting assignment and one of the German members of this multi-national salesforce had remarkable communication strengths. He was part of a sales training course that taught them, among other things, how to develop and use stories to promote their products and services. In the pre-course work he wrote one of the only stories I've ever received that I barely needed to edit. And he wrote it in English, a second language!

His communication strengths were obvious and were indicated by an assessment I had him and the others take. But when I asked him if he had ever used this story-format to promote his product, he said he had not. Why? Because he could not intentionally leverage this communication strength until he was aware he possessed it.

THE PEAK MOMENTS EXERCISE

The first tool we will use to help us understand our strengths is the Peak Moment Exercise. A peak moment occurs when you are working on something and are in the flow. Time flies by. The work may be hard, but it is not tiring. We do not dread this labor. And though the work itself is rewarding, what brings us the most joy is the result. It is a confirmation of our mastery and a source of great pride and satisfaction.

Please take a minute to think of three or more peak moments in your life. These moments need not be related to one's current line of work, but whatever it is, be sure to include the excellent results. And if your peak moment produced less than excellent results, then it might not qualify, because we are trying to find areas where you can exercise skills at a near-perfect level. Such areas produce results of the highest quality. But do not despair if you can only come up with one or two peak moments. Sometimes one is enough to uncover many of the core strengths that make up your brand.

Then, once you've written down these peak moments, analyze each one and note which strengths were required to produce these results. Were you required to learn new things and become proficient in new activities? Do you relish the opportunity to learn new things and acquire new skills? Learning is a strength that undergirds many activities, and it is not a strength everyone possesses.

Did your activity require intense focus and discipline, or were you in a competition and you enjoyed the fact that you won, or exceeded everyone's expectations? Being competitive is a strength, as is being an achiever, someone who does not quit until her work is done.

I used a feminine pronoun because I was thinking of a quiet, introverted woman who I once coached. Much of the time her voice was emotionally flat, but not when she spoke of her "achiever" strength. She looked me in the eye and her tone became authoritative as she said, "I know this is a real strength of mine. I just don't quit."

When we connect with the core of our brand it inspires this sort of passion. Now what effect do you think this might have on an interviewer as she spoke about this strength? Her tone of conviction, and passionate facial expression, would have impressed the unconscious depths of his being. He would have emotionally connected with her on an essential level. After all, this was who she was, is and will be.

Now let's return to the Peak Moments Exercise. What you are looking for are patterns, strengths that stand out and perhaps produced more than one achievement. This linking the peak moment to results is critical. It not only helps us know if a certain trait is a strength, it also helps us articulate this strength, and the results it produced, to an interviewer.

Orla Castanien, a professional coach who uses the Peak Moments Exercise to help clients understand their strengths, told me the story of a lawyer who was no longer interested in her profession during our radio interview.[3] Being a lawyer was becoming a chore that drained her. This is what happens when our work does not align with our preferences and strengths.

Orla described the Peak Moments Exercise to her and she quickly replied, "That's easy. My peak moment was planning for my wedding." She loved the logistics, the detailed planning process,

---

[3] Please go to www.tompayne.com/podcasts.html for a free, downloadable podcast of my interview with Orla.

the organization of the hundreds of details, and took special joy in the end result. In this instance, one peak moment revealed a host of strengths. She then changed her career to one that used these strengths.

Job satisfaction. If you want to generate your best possible achievements and enjoy your work, then you will need to do what Orla's client did: Find a job that aligns with your strengths. Circumstances might force you to accept a job that is less than an ideal fit, but that does not mean that a job that suits your strengths is not in your long-term plans.

DISCOVERING STRENGTHS THROUGH ACHIEVEMENTS

The Peak Moments Exercise helps you discover strengths through your passions. In this exercise you will find your strengths by working backwards from your achievements.

You start this exercise by listing three or more of your most significant achievements. These results are ones that were likely noticed by others, required time and effort, and were not commonplace.

Many people struggle with this exercise. They tend to diminish the importance of the results they produced. For example, I was helping a team of European clinical researchers to understand and leverage their strengths (among many other things), and one of the people I was coaching thought her achievements were small to non-existent. When I told her that her boss thought she was one of his most experienced, senior researchers she refused to believe it. I was stunned. I then pointed out that she was in charge of a clinical trial that was strategically vital to the company. She could not argue against that because that fact was obvious even to her, but she had to think about it to make sure I wasn't overstating things.

We see what we expect to see, and if we regularly engage in negative self-talk, then we will see insignificance when the reality is the opposite. So, if you are having this conversation with yourself, "When am I ever going to do anything important," then please stop it. The conversation will only produce bad things and it is untrue 99.9% of the time. We will return to this important topic at the end of this book.

To help clear this negative-mindset-hurdle, think in terms of your job description. What did your past jobs require you to do? List the various requirements, then, one by one, answer the question, "Did I do this?" If you did, then guess what? You accomplished things that were significant to your job.

You now have achievements, but were they the result of your strengths? Did you enjoy doing them? Or were there certain activities that you enjoyed more than others? Why did you enjoy these activities and what strengths were required to achieve this result?

I'll give you an example of how a job that is a poor fit can still reveal strengths.

BURN OUT

My desire to be a super soldier was kept alive by youthful energy, a high need-to-achieve, and ignorance. But after three years of hard work as an Airborne-Ranger qualified Infantry officer I could no longer rationalize away a stubborn fact: I was a horrible fit for my job.

The Infantry officer's job is extremely extraverted. You are outdoors much of the time and your attention is always directed to the outside world, the world of the potential threat, and to your immediate surroundings. But I was and am an introvert, so, instead of energizing me, my work was draining my energy away.

Then one day, during an exercise at the National Training Center (NTC) in Fort Irwin, California, I was given the task of developing a travel plan that would cover how our battalion's tracked vehicles would move from Point A to Point B. I was handed a fairly complex manual detailing all of the necessary parts of the plan and I quickly put one together. I enjoyed the work. It was challenging, new and required thoughtful, introverted work.

The NTC evaluators said it was one of the better travel plans they had seen, and that makes sense. It engaged what I've since discovered is my number one strength: Strategic, or the ability to quickly sort through the inessential, recognize the essential, to see patterns where others see chaos, and to use this information to develop the best plan to achieve a goal. It also engaged my analytical and learning strengths.

You may be in a job you hate, but you still may enjoy parts of your job. If so, then these areas of satisfaction can offer rich insights into what your true strengths are.

The Army was the most practical, rooted in the past, SOP-driven organization imaginable, and my mind naturally moves toward challenging the existing order to find better ways of doing things. This would not lead to my peaceful coexistence with the Army, but the Army was not the problem. It did not need to change. I did, by finding another line of work. You may be in a similar situation. If so, then I hope the words I heard at a seminar have the same impact on you as they did on me.

THE INSIGHTFUL SEMINAR

I was stationed at Fort Polk and one day got a letter from a headhunter inviting me and other officers to a seminar on job opportunities outside of the military. His words were perspective altering and life changing:

> If you love your military job and look forward to going to work the next day, then I have a question for you, "Why are you here?" You are welcome to stay and listen to what I have to say, but I advise you to remain a U.S. Army officer. You are very fortunate to like what you do for a living.
>
> But if Army life is wearing you out, if you dislike your job, then I advise you to consider leaving the military.
>
> Why? Because it is highly doubtful you will excel at a job you dislike. And if you are a bad fit for the Army, then as the days turn into years you will come to hate your job, do it poorly, and either leave five years later than you should have, or be forced to leave.

When our nature is poorly aligned with our career requirements, then misery and diminishing productivity will be the outcome.

I will now cover two assessment tools that help us to understand our strengths, the nature of our unique brand.

ASSESSMENTS: MYERS-BRIGGS

The Myers-Briggs Type Indicator® is the most widely used assessment tool there is. Over two million people take this assessment annually. It is based on Carl Gustav Jung's Type theory, which produced three dichotomies.

Type theory began with the now familiar introversion-extraversion dichotomy. But Jung began to wonder if his theory was fatally flawed, because of the extreme variations amongst introverts and extraverts. To account for this variation, he added two other dichotomies: sensing-intuition, and thinking-feeling. The mother-daughter team of Katherine Briggs and Isabel Myers then added a fourth dichotomy: judging-perceiving. They are listed below, along with a brief description:

1. **E**xtraversion-**I**ntroversion (E-I): Extraverts have an external orientation that draws energy from interacting with others, or the outside world. Introverts draw energy from operating within the internal world of thought.
2. **S**ensing-**IN**tuition (S-N): This dichotomy is concerned with the way you perceive the world. Sensing types perceive the world through their senses. They are practical and focused in the here and now. They trust the tried and true. Intuitives also perceive the world through their senses, but then use the information gathered to perceive patterns that extend out into the future. They embrace change and new approaches.
3. **T**hinking-**F**eeling (T-F): This dichotomy is about how one makes decisions. Thinking types are more impersonal, logical, and driven by what is fair and just. The Feeling types make decisions based on values and the impact of the decision on others. They tend to pursue group harmony.
4. **J**udging-**P**erceiving (J-P): This dichotomy is based, in large part, on a preference toward completing tasks. The judger prefers to finish tasks and is energized thereby. The

perceiver likes to keep things open until the deadline approaches, something that energizes them.

Depending on your preference, each of these areas produces a letter in your four-letter type. If you are an Introvert (I) who perceives via the Intuition (N), makes decisions through Thinking (T), and are a Judging (J) type, who prefers finishing tasks to leaving them open-ended, then you are an INTJ. This is my type and when I discovered this it gave me insights into those strengths of mine that I can leverage.

The MBTI® approach contends that each individual is the ultimate decider of his or her type. The assessment's outcome is not authoritative. Typically it is correct in all four letters only 60% to 80% of the time, depending on the study, and some view this as a fatal flaw that discredits the entire system. I disagree. I think it is a reflection of our confusion over what we prefer, our strengths, and who we are.

For example, my military and sales careers were two extremely extraverted professions, and I was initially assessed as an ENTJ, an extravert rather than an introvert. I was answering the assessment's questions based on the perspective of who I was at work rather than who I actually was. Because of the possibility of type confusion, a certified instructor takes the assessed person through several exercises to confirm their best-fit type.

I use this assessment in my management consulting practice to help people understand how they and others have unique preferences that need to be embraced, because their differences are valuable to the team's performance. And also to help organizations, and jobseekers, understand what their strengths and weaknesses are.

STRENGTHSFINDER

This is another assessment tool that I use because it is strength-specific. In its more expensive version, this assessment rank orders your thirty-four strengths from one through thirty-four, while its less-expensive option offers you your top five strengths.[4]

The table below is a tool I use to help clients understand what strengths they are using to produce results. It notes a significant achievement and their top five strengths as determined by the StrengthsFinder assessment. It then asks them to weight how much each strength was engaged in the production of this result.

In the example below, Jill, our previously introduced VP of Manufacturing, achieved a 100-fold improvement in quality. Three of her strengths—communication, futuristic, and activator—were fully engaged by this task.[5] If these same strengths kept reappearing in the achievement of other tasks, then Jill would know what her core strengths are, and the sort of results they produce. This information would serve as the basis of her branding statement. At this early stage it might appear as follows: I am an influential communicator who can paint such a compelling vision of the future that it gets people to move toward its achievement.

Achievement	Strength	Weight
1. Instituted new manufacturing processes that led to a 100-fold reduction of errors.	a. Individualization	4
	b. Communication	10
	c. Futuristic	8
	d. Learner	3
	e. Activator	9

---

[4] At the time of this writing the assessments are available at www.gallupstrengthscenter.com for $89.99 and $9.99.
[5] The communication strength enables people to put their thoughts into words with ease and efficacy. They typically have conversational and presenting skills. Futuristic people find inspiration in future possibilities and are able to inspire others with their vision of the future. Activators are often impatient people who can turn thoughts into action. They make things happen.

This table also tells another story. Jill has strengths that aren't being utilized as completely as they should. Is she tailoring her communication toward individuals in her team, and using her knowledge of their strengths to engage them in different ways? Or, stated differently, is she leveraging her individualization strength as fully as she should? This part of the self-discovery process might not help her in an interview, since this strength does not point to results, but it could help her achieve bigger and better results in her next job, and also in her job search preparations.

For example, Jill could look at critical activities like networking, developing a branding statement and stories, and see if she was fully utilizing her strengths to do a better job at these job search tasks. Let's say she has a networking goal of making at least five networking calls a week with the intent of generating ten additional networking leads from these five contacts, but she is failing to reach this goal, week after week.

When she looks at her strengths she realizes that she has done a poor job of research on people she is calling (individualization), and has not spent enough time on developing a script for her calls (an underutilization of her communication strength). She has also failed to learn much about the industries and companies of her networking contacts, or about the networking process (learner). By using these strengths she will be more effective at this networking task, and her strengths are preferred activities that she does well.

Goal	Strength	Weight
1. Networking target of 5 new contacts per week. Generating ten new networking contacts.	a. Individualization	3
	b. Communication	5
	c. Futuristic	9
	d. Learner	6
	e. Activator	9

Jill has begun to walk down the path of intentionally engaging her strengths, a path that would benefit anyone. Most people use their strengths accidentally, and this diminishes the results they can achieve, the success they can enjoy, and job satisfaction. Job search is about more than merely finding another job. It is about self-discovery, and then putting this hard-won knowledge to use both during and after the conclusion of the job-search process.

PREFERENCES, STRENGTHS, SATISFACTION

Zappos wants to offer its customers exceptional service over the phone. It makes its toll-free number readily available on every page of its website. Zappos understands that its job requires a unique personality. Not everyone is cut out for phone work, day after day. But here is the problem: If they hire someone who is not a good fit for the job, then this person will likely perform poorly for weeks or months, before being counseled, coached, and let go.

This not only hurts Zappo's ability to deliver consistent, superior customer service, it is also costly. To prevent this from occurring they tell their trainees, who have just completed their four-week training program, that they will receive full pay for their four weeks of training, and an additional $1,000 if they will quit. It is called the offer.

The offer is based on this belief: After four weeks of training the potential employee must have a pretty good idea about whether or not they want to take on this job. Either it is a good fit or it isn't. For those who enjoy the work, the four-weeks of pay, plus $1,000, is hardly enough to get them to quit, but for those who don't like the energy-draining stress of a job that is a poor fit, the money is a strong incentive to leave.

The point of the Zappos story is simple. We have strengths that enable us to be engaged and satisfied in certain lines of work, but not in others. Our strengths produce results and we need to know them, and be able to articulate them, in order to secure those opportunities that fit and lead to job satisfaction.

In the next chapter we will learn how to create a branding statement that can be used in networking, informational interviewing, answering the question "Tell me about yourself," and can also appear as your "Summary of Qualifications" at the top of your resume. This makes the branding statement a versatile, job-search tool that can help us achieve the goal of repetition with variation.

10

The Branding Statement

THE ENDLESS ANSWER

She was a top talent, and like most of my clients—at least at first—she was incapable of talking about herself in a compelling way. Making matters worse, she was unaware of this shortcoming. Few things could illustrate this more clearly than the way she answered the question, "Will you tell me about yourself?" Her slow moving, train wreck of an answer rolled down and off the tracks as follows:

> Me: Do you have different, customized answers to the question, "Tell me about yourself"?
>
> Her: I do.
>
> Me: Good. How many versions?
>
> Her: Three.
>
> Me: How do you decide which one to use?
>
> Her: Well that can be tough. On my last interview I started with my favorite version. But as I was getting toward the end I thought, "My second favorite is also really good." So I added my second version to the first. Then, as I was getting near the end…

Me: You didn't add in the third one, did you?

Her: I did.

She must have thought, "She who presents the most reasons and the best reasons wins." But she failed to realize that the data-dump is where interviews go to die.

I imagined a stressed interviewer sitting across from her for four minutes, or more, wondering when this verbal simulation of waterboarding would end. It eventually did, as did her interviewing for this opportunity.

There is a better way. This chapter will show you how to develop an answer to this question that works.

"BREVITY IS THE SOUL OF WIT"[1]

When I was interviewing job-search experts for a radio program, I had the good fortune of working with a radio-producing legend, Lorna Gladstone. Her vast experience gave her an instinctual understanding of radio, and one of the many lessons she taught me was to keep my guest's answers to one minute, or seventy-five seconds at most. When you have one person speaking for ninety seconds or more, you start to lose the interest-generating give-and-take of the radio interview.

This rule applies to keeping the interviewer engaged as well. Two minutes of densely packed greatness is a lot to digest. It can lead to wandering minds that eventually check out completely.

One of the reasons jobseekers ramble endlessly in response to the "Tell me about yourself" question is because writing out an answer, editing it several times, timing it, then rehearsing and memorizing it, is hard work. But few tasks are more important. If you cannot articulate your strength in a compelling way, then your success is based on the hope that your competitors will be equally ill prepared.

You will likely be amazed at how much information can be fit into

---

[1] William Shakespeare, *Hamlet*, Act 2, Scene 2, l. 90. In the context of Polonius's discourse, "wit" means "acumen," or "sound judgment."

a seventy-five second answer. But whatever you do, whatever path you choose to walk upon, please remember: Data dumps are a job search crime punishable by rejection. Avoid this failed approach and embrace the clear and concise style of the branding statement.

PART ONE: THE BRANDING SENTENCE

We begin this process by developing a list of our core strengths and the results they've produced. Once completed, we set ourselves the following goal:

> I will create a sentence that contains the strengths most relevant to the hiring organization, and sums up my potential value to them. It will also serve as a hook, a way of grabbing their attention and making them want to know more.

Here is an example of a salesperson's branding sentence. His research has uncovered that his primary role at the hiring company will be increasing revenue through the management of strategic accounts. The phrase, "It's a relationship business," keeps appearing in the company's interviews and blog posts. He uses this knowledge to customize his branding statement to highlight his relationship-building strengths. This will make the entire branding statement seem less like a sales pitch and more like the addressing of a need, a solution to the problem of hiring a good fit.

When asked, "Tell me about yourself," he begins with his branding sentence, "I am one of Acmecom's top-five salespeople in the country, and I got there by developing relationships with customers that are so strong, they became my volunteer salesforce."

If I am the interviewer I'm hooked. I want to know more. I wonder, "How can customers become his volunteer salesforce? Could it be possible that our relationship-building strength could be taken to another level?"

In one sentence he has defined his brand. It is in line with the values and strengths of the hiring organization, and the rest of his answer will make his brand come alive.

A customer service manager might say, "I am a customer service manager and I coach my team to provide a level of service that makes our customers customers-for-life."

I want to know how this customer service manager turns customers into customers for life. What is she coaching her team to do? I am hooked.

Now imagine you are at a networking meeting and someone asks, "What is it you do?" And you reply, "I am a salesperson who has discovered the secret to sales success: [Pause.] Get your customers to sell for you."

This modified branding sentence drops the emphasis on relationship building because the values of the networking contact are unknown. Relationship building may resonate powerfully with this person or it may fall flat. He could be more task-oriented than people-oriented. But this branding sentence still seeks to hook his attention and open the door for additional conversation about the value this salesperson can bring a company. A businessperson would likely want to know more about this secret to sales success. This longer conversation could then lead to new networking contacts or even employment.

For the record, it took me only a few moments to come up with my branding sentence. But it took several months to refine it into what it has now become: "I am a management consultant who makes organizations more successful by aligning business practices with human nature."

Is it great? No, but it does tell what I do and it typically hooks the attention of the person with whom I am speaking. He often wants to know what this "aligning business practices with human nature" is all about. I am then granted the opportunity of speaking at greater length about what I do.

The above branding sentence that I created for a fictitious salesperson is another example of how this process can take weeks and sometimes months of refinement. It went through over a dozen re-writes. This extensive editing process points to a guideline related to the creative problem-solving process.

QUANTITY

When I am conducting workshops with corporate staffs I will ask them to write their three best sentences using three words. Almost any three words will work. For example, "green," "line," "cold." And then sentences will come out like, "The line to get green, cold cash from the ATM was five minutes long and getting longer." "I drew a green line across the cold, white snow and dared the opposing team to cross it," and so on.

After we finish I ask, "How many sentences did you come up with?" They look at me slightly puzzled and say, "Three. You asked for three."

I reply, "I asked for your three best sentences. Research shows that the commonplace, least creative sentences are the ones that appear first. But the more creative ones appear later, after the obvious sentences are exhausted."

And so it is with the branding sentence. Write it down. Write another, another and another. Write until they become difficult to come up with, and then take some of the best elements of what you've come up with to create your best sentence. Ask yourself, "Does this sum up the value I can bring to hiring organizations?" And, as importantly, "Would this make the hiring authority want to know more? Does it hook their attention?"

PART TWO: STORIED ACHIEVEMENTS

The branding sentence is followed by achievements that appear in a shortened story format. We will build on the salesperson's branding sentence and show how the achievements reinforce the brand.

> *Branding Sentence*:
>
> I am one of Acmecom's top-five salespeople in the country, and I got there by developing relationships with customers that are so strong, they became my volunteer salesforce.
>
> *Storied Achievements*:
>
> It works like this: I took a major, prospective customer,

Acme, on a site visit to show them how our system was being used. Then, because of the strength of my relationships, I left Acme alone with my customers. They then told Acme how I was not just a salesperson, I was a valued part of their team. They described how I visited them weekly to custom configure their system and make it the best possible solution. They sold Acme, and since they have a credibility no salesperson can have, they became our company's strongest and best salesperson.

I then took the time to understand Acme's needs and work with them to fine-tune a solution that was perfect. Acme is now a $2,000,000 account, one of our largest, and I am a valued part of their team. Best of all, they are one of my strongest, most vocal salespeople.

The second part sometimes consists of one achievement or two. It is difficult to deliver three achievements within the time constraints, but sometimes this can be done. The goal is not quantity of information, because too much information causes mental indigestion. The goal is emotional impact. What can you say that delivers the maximum emotional punch?

Whenever you can add financial-impact to your branding statement, do so. This is easily done in the case of sales opportunities. But it can also be done with a manufacturing management position (cost reduction through quality control), or with a customer service position (increased customer satisfaction resulting in fewer lost customers), and with other positions as well.

Editing is essential at every stage of this script-writing process. You will need to remove unnecessary words and simplify the language for clarity. This will turn your script into a more effective and efficient tool. It will give your branding statement energy, because it quickly makes its point. It also makes the branding statement easier to memorize.

PART THREE: SKILL SETS

If there is one thing missing from answers to the question, "Tell me about yourself," it is energy. They tend to meander toward irrelevance. So, this closing section is designed to give your answer energy by stating those skill sets you possess that are attractive to the hiring company, in a rapid-fire manner, as follows:

> I am an over-achiever of sales plans, a relationship builder, a problem solver, and a valued member of my customer's team.

This would form too abrupt of an ending to your answer if it were not for the fourth and final part.

PART FOUR: REENGAGING THE INTERVIEWER

This is the briefest part of the branding statement, and it is only used when answering the question, "Tell me about yourself." It returns control of the interview back to the interviewer, and attempts to continue the conversation on the subject of your value. It asks a question that makes some interviewers smile: "Which of these areas would you like to discuss?"

It is so simple and effective that I strongly advise all to add this to the end of their answer to the question, "Tell me about yourself." You can vary the wording to suit your style. For example, you might end your branding statement with, "Is there anything I've covered that you'd like to discuss in greater detail?"

THE BRANDING STATEMENT IN FULL

When we look at the branding statement as a whole, we will find that it is about a minute long and yet it contains a wealth of information. It defines this salesperson as someone who is not a string of jobs, but a valuable, results-driven professional, who just so happens to ideally fit the hiring company's values. The entire branding statement now follows:

> I am one of Acmecom's top-five salespeople in the country, and I got there by developing relationships with customers that are so strong, they became my volunteer salesforce.
>
> It works like this: I took a major, prospective customer, Acme, on a site visit to show them how our system was being used. Then, because of the strength of my

relationships, I left Acme alone with my customers. They then told Acme how I was not a salesperson; instead, I was a valued part of their team. They described how I visited them weekly to custom configure their system and make it the best possible solution. They sold Acme, and since they have a credibility no salesperson can have, they became our company's strongest and best salesperson.

I then took the time to understand Acme's needs and work with them to fine-tune a solution that was perfect. Acme is now a $2,000,000 account, one of our largest, and I am a valued part of their team. Best of all, they are one of my strongest, most vocal salespeople.

I am an over-achiever of sales plans, a relationship builder, a problem solver, and a valued member of my customer's team.

Which of these areas would you like to discuss?

Did you notice a pattern emerging? This branding statement is repetitive and this is a good thing. "Developing relationships with my customers that are so strong," "strength of my relationships," "relationship builder," is an example of repetition with variation. It is saying the same thing three different ways.

It also repeats the theme of finding solutions: "the best possible solution," "fine-tune a solution," "I am…a problem solver."

It then continues this strategy of repetition with variation by modifying the branding statement to become the header of a resume, the first thing a reader of our resume will see.

THE SUMMARY OF QUALIFICATIONS

If our branding statement is a potent expression of our value to the hiring authority, then it deserves a prominence given to nothing else. Also, when we deliver this succinct expression of value during the interview it will benefit from the fact that this summary is likely stored in the interviewer's "map of the world"—they've read your resume—and repetition makes it more likable.

After the interview, when the resumes are looked at and the

candidates begin to blur together, yours will stand out. The hiring authority will glance over your summary and think, "Oh yeah, this was the one person who answered, 'Tell me about yourself,' in a way that didn't put me to sleep. There's something about this person...I can't put my finger on it, but...I just like her. She seems to be a great fit."

The cognitive unconscious is influencing the "rational" decisions of the hiring authority without his realizing it. This is but one example of the power of aligning job search with human nature.

The salesperson's "Summary of Qualifications" might look like this:

> A key account executive achieving four consecutive years of top-five sales finishes by turning customers into his sales team. Viewed by customers as part of their strategic, problem-solving team. An overachieving revenue- and relationship-builder.

The Summary should have a hook to it. It should make the hiring authority want to know more. It starts by establishing expertise and mastery of the sales craft. Whatever your position, or profession, make it clear that you can operate at the highest level and produce results. Then offer something intriguing that might make you different from other candidates. The goal is to stand out from the crowd, and to get the hiring authority to want to read on.

This takes time and many editing passes before we get the tone right. So, please edit your work at least five or more times before you start sending your resume hither and yon.

Understanding your strengths, linking them to achievements, and articulating them in a compelling way takes time, but it is worth the investment. Nowhere is this process more powerful than in the development of memorable stories.

11

"Tell Me a Story"

60 MINUTES

Presenting your accomplishments in a story format is the most powerful interviewing tool there is, so I am always amazed when people resist using stories.

I was working with a high-ranking banking executive who wanted nothing to do with stories. She said, "It sounds too foo-foo for me."

I replied, "I bet you do like stories. Don't you like the TV show *60 Minutes* with all of its interesting, behind-the-scenes portrayals of newsworthy events?"

She said, "Yes."

"It is one of the highest-rated shows in American TV history," I continued, "and it became a huge success by turning news into stories. This was no accident. The show's creator, Don Hewitt, lived by a simple motto that he said was contained in these four little words, 'Tell me a story.'

"When someone pitched him a possible segment he would reject it if he couldn't see the story in it. So you see, even though you are an analytical type who values facts and data, you still enjoy a good story. And there are reasons why you do, and why they are so powerful in interviews."

Some of the reasons are:

1. Stories make self-promotion palatable. The interviewer will not feel like he is being sold, and you will not feel like you are selling.
2. As we saw in chapter one, stories can make your smaller achievements seem larger than the more substantial achievements of your competitors.
3. Stories are entertaining. People, who are entertaining, are more likable than those who bore interviewers with data-dumps.
4. Stories are memorable. Most people can remember stories from their childhood.
5. Good stories hook the interviewer's attention and hold it. If you are the fourth interview of the day, this can be critical.

My belief that stories are the most powerful interviewing tool is based, in part, on my personal experience.

PERSONAL EXPERIENCE

I heard about a great opportunity: A retained recruiting firm was searching for a person to assemble, and lead, a national sales force to launch a revolutionary fetal monitor.

However, there were several large obstacles in my way. I was unemployed, had a recently spotty track record, and no experience in the field of obstetrics. I later found out about an even larger obstacle: I was up against a person who was employed and had twenty years of experience with the number one medical monitoring company in the world. Worse yet, a professor who wrote the textbook used by obstetrical medical students across the country recommended him.

The last nail in my coffin: This professor was a paid consultant working for the hiring company. Not only was he a key opinion leader in the field of obstetrics, he was also an insider at the company. It is hard to imagine a better reference.

However, I got the job. You may wonder, "How?" I wondered that myself after I heard about my competition's qualifications. So I asked, one month later, "Why did you choose me?"

The answer: "You had such great stories." A month later the stories I used to secure the hiring decision were still remembered.

STYLE TRUMPS SUBSTANCE, PERCEPTION TRUMPS REALITY

Our minds give immense power to how something is presented. It can make reality take a back seat to what is seen, heard and even tasted. One of the best illustrations of this is the way a tasteless food color can change the way food tastes.

Participants in an experiment were asked to taste dishes of the same food that were colored with a tasteless food coloring. The dishes of food tasted the same in reality, but perception, armed with its 10,000,000 visual bits of information per second, was not going to be overruled by the rational mind's forty bits.

The food may have tasted the same to blindfolded subjects of the experiment, but these participants could see. The green food was tart like an apple, the red-dyed food was sweet like a cherry, and the blue food was awful. Blue was associated with black or rotten food.

Now here is the strange part. After the subjects of the experiment were told the taste of the different plates of food was identical, they replied, "You are wrong. This tastes sweet and this tastes tart." And in a way the subjects were right. The food did taste differently to their brains.

> When tasteless yellow coloring is added to vanilla pudding, consumers say it tastes like banana or lemon pudding. ...Color creates a psychological expectation for a certain flavor that is often impossible to dislodge, Dr. Shelke said.[1]

---

[1] Gardiner Harris, *Colorless Food? We Blanch*, N. Y. Times, April 2, 2011.

We see what we expect to see, we taste what we expect to taste, and reality bends to fit perception's mandate. How you present yourself and your achievements can be more important than the reality of the achievement itself.

However, few people have the discipline to put in the work to create and memorize six or more stories. If you do, then you will have a significant advantage over your competition. By illuminating your understanding about the power of stories, I hope to motivate you to put forth the effort great stories require. Here are a few more reasons why stories are powerful:

1. Some people are more visual than others. Stories enable you to communicate more effectively to them.
2. Stories make you stand apart from your competitors who don't use this technique, or who use it ineffectively.
3. Stories are digestible. The data, or achievement, comes with context. This gives the rational mind the scale to weigh the information, and the time to appreciate it.
4. Stories are the way our minds work. When confronted with two disparate pieces of information our minds subconsciously try to produce a narrative regarding both of them that makes sense.
5. Stories lodge patterns in the cognitive unconscious, the mental system that creates and stores patterns.
6. Finally, stories are familiar. They are not novel or threatening. In fact, they enable the audience to experience real emotions within the safety of the narrative arc.

BUT MY JOB IS NOTHING SPECIAL

Stories can work well for anyone. I have worked pro bono for the Elam Davies Social Services Center in Chicago to help jobseekers develop interviewing skills.[2] They weren't your typical job-seeking

---

[2] The Elam Davies Social Services Center serves "the least, the last and the lonely" with dignity and respect and has done so since 1983. They are one of six programs operating within the Chicago Lights non-profit. If you are interested in learning more about them, then please visit

group. They faced significant barriers such as a history of drug abuse, unstable housing, and inadequate insurance. One group included a person with HIV who was also in recovery from drug addiction, and a few people lacked teeth because they could not afford proper dental care.

When I offered to help them I wondered if I could. I knew these interviewing techniques worked well at the executive level, but wondered if they would work well at their level.

It turns out they do. Stories highlighting the human condition—the struggles we all face—are moving whether they are set in the Mumbai slums of the hit movie, *Slumdog Millionaire*, or somewhere closer to home. The most menial activities can create a hook that grips the mind, charms the heart, and stays with you long after.

I still remember Sherry's story. Her job? Putting stickers on packages for a large retail chain:

> I started a job for a retail chain putting stickers on packages. The quota for each day was 1,000 and I was struggling at around 150. So were all of the other new-hires. About six of them quit after a day or two, but I don't quit. I saw someone who was overachieving her quota every day and asked her how she did it. After she showed me some of the tricks of the trade I not only made my quota, I was promoted to a higher level of responsibility.

Her touching story highlights the power of style. Let's give these same facts in a style-free manner and see if the impact is the same.

If Sherry was asked, "How have you dealt with a difficult situation in the past?" She could have answered, "I was given a very difficult quota—putting stickers on a thousand packages each day—and I sought coaching, worked hard and eventually made it. But I've got to tell you, it wasn't easy."

All that I am thinking about is her putting stickers on packages and, in my superior, condescending way, am also thinking, "How

www.chicagolights.org.

hard could that be?" But when you have the drama of working under a pressure that is crushing others, and overcoming the obstacle, then the nature of the task doesn't matter.

Like most stories, Sherry's is very versatile. It could be used to answer the following questions:

> Can you give me an example of how you have overcome adversity?
>
> What achievement are you proudest of?
>
> What are your strengths?

When answering these questions Sherry may need to modify her story by adding something at the end of it like, "As this story shows, my strengths are persistence, hard work, learning quickly while on the job and problem solving. I was faced with a difficult problem that many others couldn't solve, but I found a way to solve it."

This addition is like the moral of a story. Some stories have such an obvious message that no "moral" is necessary. But unless a moral is overkill, adding one makes sense. The interviewer may already be exhausted when you interview, and his fried brain may fail to connect the dots. Also, it is another way of employing repetition with variation.

Hopefully I've convinced you about the necessity of story creation. A story is the most powerful interviewing tool I know of, and it follows a simple formula that almost anyone can master. The next chapter will detail that formula, and give you helpful tips based on my experience of helping many others.

12

A Formula for Success

H.A.P.: HOOK, ACTIONS, PAYOFF

The key to writing a good story, and then telling it, is to follow a simple pattern. A story begins with a *hook*, a situation typically involving conflict that hooks the attention of the audience. It makes them want to hear more. It can paint a seemingly hopeless situation that makes the listener want to know, "How did he get out of that one?" or, "What happens next?"

In the second phase we detail the *actions* taken to overcome the obstacle.

The story ends with the *payoff*. What was the impact of the *actions*?

Clients of mine tend to struggle with each of these sections for different reasons. I will cover these issues in detail.

THE HOOK AND CONFLICT

"Why call it a hook?" you may wonder. Why not call it a *situation*, *challenge*, or *circumstance*, words favored by others who use this story-writing formula. I use the word "hook," because the words "situation" and "circumstance" fail to describe the mission of the first part of the story. As a result my clients initially write first drafts of stories that fail to hook the attention of me or anyone else.

What I typically see in this first part of the story are bland recollections of details that fail to paint a picture of the enormity of the obstacle, the "villain" standing in the way of the hero's success—yes, jobseeker, you will be the hero of every job-interviewing story you write. As mythologists, moviemakers and novelists know, conflict is interesting, particularly when the villain is both unique and powerful. Think about Theseus vs. the half-man, half-bull Minotaur, David vs. Goliath, Othello opposed by the cunning, remorseless Iago, and the list goes on forever.

A hook needs to turn your task, or obstacle, into as exceptional and powerful a "villain" as possible, because it makes your achievement all the more heroic and entertaining. It engages the audience and makes them want to hear the rest of the story.

Here is a "situation" or "challenge": "I was hired by Acme to lead their sales team during a time of severe financial stress." This is what I typically see, the embryo of a story that is never born. It is a "situation," not a "hook." I will listen to this story, but I am not attending to what is being said with an eager expectation about how this story might unfold. Severe financial stress must have a story behind it, and the person telling this story was an eyewitness.

By adding a few, pertinent details this "situation" can become a "hook."

> Shortly after I joined Acme they discovered accounting errors and the CFO was fired. When this was announced our stock price was cut in half in after hours trading. Then our company went through a restructuring that laid off 15% of the workforce. When analysts started to wonder out loud, "When will Acme disappear," some of our best people left. I knew I needed to generate some positive results quickly before our company ran out of time.

The hiring authority is now an insider to an unpublished story. What happened behind the scenes? How did you get out of that mess? What happened next?

Dramatic conflict is the pulsing heart of a good story. In the above example, details were added that made the obstacle—the villain of the story—larger and more daunting. I am sometimes stunned by the powerful details people fail to include in their stories.

Note also the emotional power of facts calmly stated. "Accounting errors," "stock price was cut in half," "some of our best people left," are details that need no dramatic addition. They stand on their own and create tension.

There are physiological reasons why we want to make the hook as emotionally powerful as possible. They generate a mild stress response that affects memory. I believe this is one of the reasons why my stories were remembered a month after the interview.

THE MILD STRESS RESPONSE

In this study a control group was read a story that was largely a bunch of details strung together:

> …[A] boy and his mother walk through their town, pass this store and that one, cross the street and enter the hospital where the boy's father works, are shown the X-ray room.[1]

Boring! A few weeks later this control group had difficulty remembering any of the story's details.

The experimental subjects, however, were read a similar story with a dramatic twist in the middle of it:

> …[A] boy and his mother walk through their town, pass this store and that one, cross the street where…the boy is hit by a car! He's rushed to the hospital and taken to the X-ray room.[2]

The experimental group remembered these emotionally charged details much better than the control group remembered their emotionless details.

---

[1] Sapolsky, p. 210.
[2] Sapolsky, p. 210.

It appears that a mild stress response with its release of epinephrine, norepinephrine and energy stores into the bloodstream, was behind the memorization of this story. Because when the experiment was repeated, and the experimental group had their stress response blocked by a drug used to reduce blood pressure, they could not remember the middle portion of the story with the boy being hit by the car any better than the controls remembered the middle of their story.

So, the emotionally charged hook causes a mild stress response that aids memory, and this is what we must strive to create. I'm not talking about something overly dramatic, but adding details that enhance the nature of the conflict are important.

RANK ORDERING THE SECTIONS

Whenever I ask classes to rank order the importance of each section very few say the hook is number one. All three components of a story are important, but if you don't have a hook, you don't have a story. This is because the interviewer won't listen if a story doesn't interest him, or remember it if it does not create the mild stress response that well-scripted conflict tends to generate. But if you hook the interviewer, he will want to see how your "villain" was defeated.

This makes a strong hook a necessity, so start your story-writing process by locating your career's hooks. Think about the seemingly insurmountable obstacles you've faced and overcome, your biggest challenges. They may have been stretch-goals your boss gave you, or interpersonal challenges you overcame. You may have been part of a team that overachieved, and if so, then think about the role you played and your contribution. Being a member of a successful team is a valuable skill, particularly when you are able to show how you were a productive member within it.

Think about your achievements, the ones that may have been noted in an annual review. The results that you associated with strengths probably have great storytelling material. And if you received unsolicited praise for something, then the reason for this praise probably has a story.

If you struggle to come up with hooks, then look over a list of standard interviewing questions, including behavioral questions, and answer them. Then see if any of your answers has a powerful hook that can start a good story.

Interviewers often use behavioral questions and this is good news, because stories answer these questions quite well. If you are unfamiliar with behavioral questions, a few examples are:

> Give me an example of a goal you set, or were given, and how you achieved it.

> Give me an example of a mistake you made and how you handled it.

> Give me an example of a challenge you faced and how you dealt with it.

Behavioral questions force the jobseeker to recount specific experiences or actions that show they have a sought after skill-set, or the character to handle adversity and succeed. The reason why stories make such effective answers to these types of questions is because they can place these behaviors, or actions, in the most memorable and powerful format: a story.

ACTIONS TAKEN

The *actions taken* segment needs to:
1. Logically lead to the payoff.
2. Be concrete, but not too detailed.
3. Illustrate your competence or abilities.

In Jill's manufacturing story the actions she took lead to the payoff, are concrete, and illustrate her competence:

> To turn this situation around *I developed a plan with measurable milestones* and whenever we achieved one *we would have a mini-celebration. We worked together on process improvements that built quality into the product.*

These italicized actions logically lead to the payoff and are concrete. They also illustrate her competence as a motivational leader and teambuilding skills.

Stories should not try to accomplish too much. For example, in the above actions segment she could go into her application of the six-sigma approach to drive process improvements, and many other details. But her mastery of the six-sigma process for driving quality gains is better handled by a separate story, or by a scripted answer that is clear and concise. What you want to avoid is getting bogged down with too many details. We are aiming for cognitive ease and clarity, not cognitive strain and a data dump.

A final word of advice on the actions taken section: Write down all of the important actions you took. There may be ten or more. Then pick the top three, or only those that are necessary to lead to the payoff, because too many details will overwhelm the mind. This is one of the places where stories often self-destruct.

We want to limit the number of details because the actions segment is the least important part of the story. This is because we tend to remember what is said first (the primacy effect), and what is said last (the recency effect), but forget what is said in the middle. Therefore, let this section serve its proper role as a bridge that connects the hook and payoff.

THE PAYOFF

I prefer the word "payoff" for the story's conclusion, because it illustrates what you are trying to achieve. A story's ending should reward the audience for their attention. The word "result," a descriptor favored by many for this part of the story, could be any ending, satisfying or not.

Sometimes the payoff is very short, as in the case of Sherry's story about putting stickers on packages (do you remember it?). But Jill's payoff section is much more detailed:

> Before you knew it, we became a motivated team and we reduced the failure rate 100-fold. It went from 1,000 defects per million opportunities, to ten. This resulted in annual gains of $2,000,000 to the bottom line. I'm very proud of that, but what really warms my heart is the way

our internal surveys showed my manufacturing team went from being the least satisfied employees in the company to among the most satisfied.

Is this payoff satisfying? Yes, and it is powerful because of the many emotions it generates. Jill's dysfunctional group—the company's losers—became a high-performance team. We like stories of redemption where a person, or team, rises from failure to success, and we admire those people who make a difference in the lives of others.

This story also inspires the emotion of hope, because it shows how Jill is a transformational leader and turnaround artist. This might inspire a hiring authority to think, "Imagine the impact Jill could have with our company. Our manufacturing group is middle of the pack in our surveys of satisfaction. She could make them world-beaters."

Her story inspires trust, because it shows she is competent and capable of turning a bad problem into a good solution. It quiets fears. Who would worry about having their employees reporting to her? All of these emotions are generated by one story, and emotions cause the hiring decision.

MONEY IS EMOTION QUANTIFIED

Imagine we are friends and you loan me $10, and I don't pay you back. Additionally, I ignore all of your hints and reminders to repay it. This annoys you and changes how you feel about me. It might not end our friendship, but it would be an irritant, and you would probably never loan me another nickel.

Think about that. A simple little sum of $10 generated the emotions of distrust and anger. But what if you loaned me $100,000, and I did not pay you back? Would the emotions be the same?

No. As the dollar amount increases, so does the emotional response toward non-payment. This larger amount would make you *feel* the painful blow, and the pain might grow stronger over time. The injury has gone from a slap—$10—to a gunshot wound. You might also feel betrayed, and angry enough to seek justice or, failing that, perhaps revenge.

The more money, the more emotion, because money is emotion quantified. This makes money a unique type of data that we need to include in our interview answers. Data and statistics are forgettable, but *added $2,000,000 to the bottom line* will be remembered long after the interview is over. Large amounts of money tend to generate an emotional response and the memory-enhancing, mild stress response that accompanies it.

Money also gives scale and dimension to an accomplishment. Without providing these numbers I leave the interviewer ignorant about the impact of my actions. By providing them I tell the interviewer, "My productivity will make your company money."

SATISFYING PAYOFFS

Payoffs need to be satisfying, because weak payoffs are huge let downs. Instead of a story rewarding our attention, we feel robbed. This is particularly true if the first two parts of the story are strong, and create expectations that aren't being met by the conclusion.

For example, "When I joined Acme the company had failed to grow its revenue for ten straight years. I immediately began to assess the talent of the salesforce and replaced the underachievers with overachievers. I invested heavily in training and new marketing materials. By the end of my first fiscal year with the company, Acme was growing again. It wasn't much, but one-half of one percent was the company's first sign of revenue growth in ten years." .5%! I bet that flat-line had the Board of Directors dancing in the street!

Stories like this resemble the lob in basketball. There I am soaring to the rim, the pass is in my hands as I am still ascending, I'm getting ready to throw down a thunderous dunk, and then my dunk clangs off the rim and my opponent scores.

If your story has a weak hook, or a weak ending, then throw it away. It is a liability and not an asset.

EMBEDDED STORIES

If you've ever been the one conducting interviews, then ask yourself, "What happens after the last interview of a long day?"

At day's end you might find yourself looking at the five resumes and wondering, "Who was this person? Did I interview him? Why can't I match his face to his resume?"

An important decision needs to be made, but all of the candidates are starting to blur together. They have successfully performed a disappearing act. To keep from disappearing, you need to use *repetition with variation*. For example, we can repeat the essence of our stories in the resume.

Jill's story about the 100-fold improvement in quality could reappear in her resume as follows:

- Led team from being the most dissatisfied in the company to posting the highest job-satisfaction scores and the lowest turnover rate.

- Reduced defect rate 100-fold, taking product from the lowest quality level in the industry to the highest.

- Added $2,000,000 to the bottom line by dramatically lowering the cost of manufactured goods.

We now return to the hiring authority who, at the end of a long day, has five resumes in front of him. He looks through the stack and sees the above bullet points. The narrative patterns lodged in the cognitive unconscious reappear on the resume and the conscious mind remembers the story that was told, because stories are memorable. The repetition of this information makes it safe and comfortable, and the cognitive unconscious sends this suggestion to the conscious mind, "Jill is good. Jill is the one. Hire Jill."

Each remembered story separates you from your competitors who are performing their vanishing act. When the interviews end, we want to be the high-definition image while our competitors are pixelated blurs.

HOW MANY STORIES?

How many stories you use will depend upon their power and their applicability. Would they capture the hiring authority's attention and imagination? Do they address the hiring authority's potential problems and needs? If they do, then why wouldn't you want to use such a story?

During one interview I would often use six or more stories, though I always had around ten stories ready. When clients hear this number they often say, "Ten! Won't the interviewer begin to think, 'Oh no. Not another story!' "

Not in my experience. If the stories are good and entertaining they will probably think, "Oh good! He's got such great stories." Remember, my six or seven stories per interview were what secured me the unlikely obstetrics job opportunity.

The secret to this process is keeping the stories short, about a minute in length. This makes the stories easier for you to remember, and it keeps them from becoming ten, dreaded, long, long stories. It also means that during a fifty-minute interview only ten minutes, at most, is spent answering questions with stories.

WHERE STORIES STAND OR FALL

Jobseekers need to spend time editing their stories prior to sharing them with a hiring authority. Stories are weak in the first-draft phase. In the next chapter we will go over the most important, and most difficult stage of the story writing process: editing.

13

The Making of a Story

DECEPTIVELY SIMPLE

There are barriers to entry in business. If the barriers to entry are low, then there will be many competitors in that space. For example, nail shops that offer manicures and pedicures are everywhere, because the barriers to entering this business are low. But there is only one company in the U.S. that makes aircraft carriers, because the barriers to entry are extremely high. There are very few countries, much less companies, that have the ability to build an aircraft carrier.

One of the beauties of using stories is the way the barrier to entry is higher than most people expect. Few take the time, or exert the effort to write, edit and remember a good story.

Stories seem so simple that job-seeking clients assume they are easy. And that's where most people stumble. They equate simple with easy. But the following paragraph, written by the previously introduced, excellent prose stylist, William Zinsser, shows how difficult good writing can be. This is his description of a reader who is struggling to understand something that is poorly written:

> Faced with such a variety of obstacles, the reader is at first a remarkably tenacious bird. He tends to blame himself. He

obviously missed something, he thinks, and he goes back over the mystifying sentence, or over the whole paragraph, piecing it out like an ancient rune, making guesses and moving on. But he won't do this for long. He will soon run out of patience. The writer is making him work too hard—harder than he should have to work—and the reader will look for a writer who is better at his craft.[1]

What do you think of the quality of his writing? Is his paragraph well written or poorly written? When I first read it I thought, "Pretty good," and I still think that. After all, as he notes in his book, *On Writing Well: An Informal Guide to Writing Non-Fiction*, this paragraph was rewritten four or five times.

Now look at the number of changes he made in his final rewrite. The following heavily annotated version is to help you visualize the number of deleted words, phrases and other changes he made, and a final, easier-to-read draft, without the editing notations, will appear below:

> Faced with [these] ~~such a variety of~~ obstacles, the reader is at first a remarkably tenacious bird. He ~~tends to~~ blame[s] himself [--] H he obviously missed something, ~~he thinks,~~ and he goes back over the mystifying sentence, or over the whole paragraph, piecing it out like an ancient rune, making guesses and moving on. But he won't do this for long. ~~He will soon run out of patience.~~ The writer is making him work too hard—~~harder than he should have to work~~—and the reader will look for ~~a writer~~ [one] who is better at his craft.[2]

---

[1] William Zinsser, *On Writing Well: An Informal Guide to Writing Non-Fiction* (New York: Harper & Row, Publishers, Inc., 1985), pp. 10-11. Please note that this quotation is slightly changed from the original as it appears in the book. The book has an image of two typewritten manuscript pages with his handwritten editing notes on them. I am sharing his fourth or fifth draft without corrections in this quote. The quotation that follows will show *typewritten* corrections, followed by the final draft as it appears in the book.

[2] Zinsser, pp. 10-11.

He has so many edits on this final draft that it looks like he was working from a first draft instead of his fourth or fifth. And he was a very good writer!

Now here is the final corrected copy. He has gone from ninety-five to seventy-three words. That is a 23% reduction on a fifth or sixth draft! The result is a better-written paragraph that is lean and clean, which is what our writing must aim for:

> Faced with these obstacles, the reader is at first a remarkably tenacious bird. He blames himself—he obviously missed something, and he goes back over the mystifying sentence, or over the whole paragraph, piecing it out like an ancient rune, making guesses and moving on. But he won't do this for long. The writer is making him work too hard, and the reader will look for one who is better at his craft.[3]

Also note, the grade level of this excellent piece of prose is 8.1, and the readability is well above the 60 mark at 68.9. In other words, a beautiful writing style is easy to understand.

THE DIFFICULT TASK OF WRITING

When I first read this some time ago, it was a revelation. Extensive editing is a vital part of the creative writing process, and Mr. Zinsser's editing approach offers some valuable tips:

> With each rewrite I try to make what I have written tighter, stronger and more precise, eliminating every element that is not doing useful work. Then I go over it once more, reading it aloud, and am always amazed at how much clutter can still be cut.[4]

Some people are gifted in this area of editing and writing, though they are few and far between. So what can you do if you are not one of them? Here are a few strategies you can pursue.

Number one, seek the help of someone you know who is a good

---

[3] Zinsser, p. 12.
[4] Zinsser, pp. 11.

writer. Ask them to go over your stories, but only after you've done several editing passes. There are few things more irritating than being asked to fix someone's impossible mess. It is like asking, "Would you please spend several hours of your free time to create something out of nothing?" If you want and need help, then produce something that can be helped.

If this option is not available, then you can try doing the best you can. That may sound like a daunting task, but it need not be. Focus on three things: First, eliminate the unnecessary words and phrases. Your goal is to cut your first draft in half. Second, add details that make the hook's obstacle bigger and the payoff more satisfying. And third, eliminate unnecessary details from the actions section.

You can invest in a writing guide and apply its lessons to your work. The best guide I've found is Strunk and White's *The Elements of Style*. It is a short book packed with helpful guidelines and it communicates the power of an effective writing style as well as any book I've read.

The more expensive option is to hire someone who is experienced in this area to help you. The product will likely be better, and you will probably feel more confident using this material. But, as I warn private clients of mine, if you are not willing to put in the hard work, then don't retain me, or anyone else, because you will be throwing away your money. The client must develop the first draft, because he is the only person who knows it. Then he must look at the editing changes to see if they suit his voice, and once they do, he must rehearse them many times until they can be said in a way that seems unrehearsed. This takes a lot of work and many are unwilling to work this hard.

THE FIRST DRAFT

To illustrate this editing process I wrote the first draft of a story about an achievement. It could be used to answer any number of interview questions, for example:

    Can you give me an example of your leadership style?

Have you ever coached someone in a way that improved his or her performance?

You mention teambuilding on your resume. What have you done to build up or strengthen your team?

It's not a terrible first draft—I have seen much worse—but it is in need of a lot of work:

HOOK

I had a Region Manager who was being thrown out of hospitals and not allowed to return. He was losing established, large accounts. He was also posting declining numbers. He was nearing retirement, but I was given the authority to terminate his employment. I did not want to do this for a variety of reasons so I elected to make him a sales-performance-coaching candidate.

ACTIONS

I traveled with him to see what he was doing that was making people so angry they banned him from entering their account, and I noticed how he was unconsciously responding to a customer's legitimate questions in a belittling way. So I brought this to his attention, modeled some more effective approaches to answering questions and I never witnessed this problem, or even heard of it surfacing, again.

The next step was to teach him the art of differentiation, or comparing the competitor's product to yours in a way that favors your product and is inoffensive. I showed him a differentiation presentation I used, went over it with him, and then he added these slides to his presentation. The very next day he closed a big sale and differentiated perfectly.

PAYOFF

Within two years his numbers had improved to the point where he became our Region Manager of the Year.

EVALUATION

When we create our first draft we cannot pronounce, "It is good," because it is not. It is fat with empty words and unnecessary phrases. So the next step is to cut the first draft's number of words in half. We want our final draft to be lean and muscular.

The first question we ask is, "Does the first paragraph set the hook? Does it create dramatic tension by clearly illustrating a difficult obstacle, the all-important villain of the story?"

The answer is, "It's not too bad." It tells the story of a man who is in his sixties and is performing so poorly that firing him is now not only an option, but an act of corporate self-defense. This outcome was unwanted, but his region could only hemorrhage money for so long before it was bled dry.

The obstacle is daunting. It takes on the challenge, "You can't teach an old dog new tricks." However, this obstacle still needs strengthening. One of its weaknesses is the way it meanders toward its objective. But after five, or more, editing passes I was able to reduce the number of words by more than 50%, and it made the hook stronger and clearer:

> I had a Region Manager who was nearing retirement, but was also losing large accounts and being banned from hospitals. I needed to either turn him around or fire him.

We don't want the interviewer to struggle to understand our story, or cognitively strain their mind. By removing clutter we make the story easier to follow, and clarity leads to cognitive ease. The Flesch Reading Ease score improved from 53.7, in the first draft, to 64.7 in the final version.

Clarity is important, but so is energy. By cutting out unnecessary words you give your writing an energy it likely lacks in your first draft. Instead of plodding toward its objective, it races.

ACTIONS

The second section—Actions—was filled with verbal clutter. It often is. We know what we did and we remember every unnecessary detail. Cleaning up this section was one of my most important editing duties, because there was far too much fat in this section. Editing's goal of "addition by subtraction" improved the story dramatically:

> So I travelled with him and found out why he was being banned from hospitals. On two occasions he belittled the questions customers asked and was unaware he was doing so. This problem stopped after coaching him.
>
> I then showed him how to differentiate our product and added these slides to his presentation. The next day he differentiated perfectly and closed a big sale.

The first draft of the "actions" was 128 words. It is now 64 words. This process illustrates why we must write down our stories and edit them several times. Because when we tell a story off the top of our heads we ramble on like a bad first draft. And in the interview this extemporaneous first draft is even worse than a written one, because we are composing our story on the fly under extreme pressure.

Our wordiness makes a story harder to understand and enjoy. In the first draft this section scored a 48.9 in reading ease and had a 12th grade reading level. It was far too difficult to understand. In the edited version the readability score improved to 70.9 and the grade level to 6.5. It is amazing what cutting out fat and editing can do to improve clarity.

These two sentences give you a sense of editing's impact. Here is the first draft:

> So I brought this to his attention, modeled some more effective approaches to answering questions and I never witnessed this problem, or even heard of it surfacing, again.

And here is the final draft:

> This problem stopped after coaching him.

First drafts tend to have several areas that are exceptionally lame, and this was one of them. The readability improved from 42.4—hard to understand—to 73.8, and the grade level went from 12.0 to

4.4. A fourth grader could understand this sentence, but it doesn't sound like one that was yanked from a children's book.

PAYOFF

The final section is the shortest, but it still can be made much shorter. It goes from, "Within two years his numbers had improved to the point where he became our Region Manager of the Year." To, "Two years later he was Region Manager of the Year."

This shortest of sections goes from nineteen words to ten. Is it necessary to say, "His numbers had improved to the point...."? Would he be getting Region Manager of the Year if his numbers declined? Superfluous words keep us from getting to the point.

THE CAUSE OF THE HIRING DECISION EFFECT

The final step involves adding details that give our story a greater emotional impact. The first draft may not have them, and removing words and phrases will not add them. Emotion is the language of the cognitive unconscious, and our stories need to speak this language during the interview.

The story, as it now stands, is two-dimensional. It is like an Egyptian hieroglyph. We need to give it a third dimension by humanizing it. Why, for example, did I not want to fire Joe? He was a dud, so why not replace him with a performer?

What made his termination so difficult was the way he was so likable. Joe was a great guy and this made the thought of firing him painful. Somehow this emotion needs to enter the story because it introduces an internal layer of conflict, and conflict is interesting. We want to try and make the interviewer care about Joe's fate, much as I did, and to make the PAYOFF more satisfying.

This human, emotional element is added in the bold print:

> **Joe was the best-liked** Region Manager **on my team. He was funny, kind, and** nearing retirement. He was also losing large accounts, and being banned from hospitals. I needed to either turn him around or fire him.

So I travelled with him and found out why he was being banned from hospitals. On two occasions he belittled the questions customers asked and was unaware he was doing so. **This was completely out of character, and** this problem stopped after coaching him.

I then showed him how to differentiate our product and added these slides to his presentation. **Differentiation is not an easy skill to master, but after only one class Joe said he thought he could do it.** The next day he differentiated perfectly and closed a big sale.

Two years later Joe was Region Manager of the Year. **He took three of his distributors into the rare million-dollar club and had the highest sales-penetration level in the country. When I gave him his award he got a standing ovation from the entire company. This had never happened at previous award ceremonies.**

The achievement, turning a struggling sixty-plus-year-old sales manager around, is good by itself, but in the story format it seems bigger. It also feels natural, unforced, and not like I am trying to sell someone. I'm just telling a story. The familiarity of the story format helps to create cognitive ease. The rational mind relaxes its guard and a powerful narrative pattern now lodges in the interviewer's cognitive unconscious. And it took less than one minute to tell it.

A final note on this story: I rewrote it many times prior to including it in my book *No Medal for Second Place*. Then when I looked at it for possible inclusion in this book, I saw the need for additional improvements, like quantifying the payoff, something missing in the previous version.

This task of editing one's work can go on forever, because our work will never be perfect. Thankfully, perfection is not our goal. Instead of perfection, we seek a quality level that is effective, because perfect writing is not needed to cause the hiring-decision-effect.

In the next chapter we will look at ways to promote our abilities without appearing to sell. This approach will feel much more natural to you and the hiring authority than the simple sales approach that focuses on delivering one feature after another.

14

Become the Solution

TO SELL WITHOUT SELLING

Our goal is to promote our brand without appearing to sell. How can this be done? We've already covered stories, and how they don't feel like selling. But how else can we move away from the ineffective, simple sales model?

Do you remember the high-level hospital officer who once said to me, "I've been here two days and you've yet to try to sell me anything"? Her story offers us a guideline for developing our answers.

She did not feel like I was selling her because I was discussing problems that were annoying to her and her staff, and potential solutions. I was looking at her world through her eyes. This approach was emotionally powerful, because as I discussed their problems their minds were put in touch with this source of pain. They relived this painful experience as they remembered it. This made the solutions I offered seem even more powerful and desirable. It also made them more memorable. By reawakening a painful memory I was creating a mild stress response that assists memory formation.

THE SOLUTION

To experience the power of this technique, imagine a problem that you now have that is extremely annoying. It could be your next-door neighbor has an annoying dog that barks at all hours. It's driving you crazy.

Now imagine I have a subsonic device that automatically emits a tone whenever the dog barks that conditions the dog to stop barking. With this device in hand, I come up to you and say, "I understand you have a dog next door that barks and barks and barks at all hours."

The emotion-laden memory of the problem, and the irritation it has caused, is brought to the forefront of your mind. I then add, "I can make this problem go away." And then I demonstrate the solution and it works.

At that moment, would I appear to be a salesperson, or a solution to an aggravating problem? I would probably appear to be a solution, someone who could remove a big stressor from your life. That is the way the nursing officer saw our product and the team presenting it. And she bought our product even though we failed to sell her for one moment, according to her.

To make our answers as effective as possible, we need to uncover what they need, their problems or sources of pain. What are they hoping to find in a candidate? And what do they really need, but do not yet know they need? More on that in a moment.

Once we know this, we can determine whether our unique strengths are a good fit for this opportunity. Can our strengths be used to solve the hiring company's problems? In short, can we become the solution?

If we cannot, if our strengths don't match their needs, then do we really want a job that will fail to engage that which we do consistently at a near-perfect level. And do we want to do something that we can't see ourselves doing repeatedly, successfully and enjoyably?[1]

Jobs that fail to engage our strengths are the ones where years of service are measured in dog years. Your first year feels like seven. But if it is a fit, then we will be able to illustrate how we are a perfect fit much more easily after having gone through this exercise.

THE COMPANY'S SITUATION

Finding out what a hiring company needs requires a little research, and we can start by understanding their situation. Are they growing rapidly? Then, prior to the interview, Google-search the problems rapidly growing companies face. One of them is eroding customer service. The backend support systems may struggle to keep up, and salespeople may be in such high-demand that they cannot visit all of the customers who request a visit.

Also, Google the problems faced by the company you are interviewing with. If they have a high enough profile, then there may be specific issues challenging them that are shared online.

How can you use this information? If it is likely that their support systems are struggling to keep up with growth, and you are in operations, then stories about how you improved productivity to achieve higher levels of customer satisfaction would be good ones to tell. It would show how hiring you is a solution to a problem they are probably facing.

Is the company trying to stage a business turnaround? This challenge brings a host of different challenges. Again Google-search these problems and see if your strengths provide possible solutions.

Oftentimes a business turnaround involves a leadership change. If a company has a new CEO, then what is his vision for the company's future? Do your strengths provide ways to advance the company toward the realization of that vision?

You want to be the solution to their problems, but you also want to

---

[1] This is Marcus Buckingham's definition of a strength.

be a good fit. As you research the company, look for the way it markets its brand. Do they position themselves as an innovative brand, and does it actually have a reputation for innovation? And, if they are innovators, how do your strengths align with theirs? What have you done that was creative and new?

Or is their focus on quality? Do you have a track record of improving quality? Perhaps they emphasize both.

Look for patterns that emerge from their blog posts, from CEO interviews, and their website. How well do your strengths, and the results you've driven, align with these emerging patterns?

What are their values and the things they value most? Is this a good fit with your values?

WHAT THE COMPANY SAYS IT NEEDS

Another part of the research involves understanding what they say they are looking for. This appears in their job description. I will use one picked at random from LinkedIn® to show how they can reveal what a company is looking for.

The job description I chose starts with two paragraphs telling me how great the company is. In their attempt to attract top talent, the company is wisely trying to sell whoever is qualified and interested in the opportunity. Though you may be tempted to skip over this section, don't. It can reveal something important about their core values.

The company that posted this job description is a well-known industrial giant, and their self-description emphasized something I never would have expected. Namely, they are fiercely committed to going "green." This information would lead me to develop "green" answers to questions. For example, my answer to a question about how I handled a challenge might involve the way I got my last company to reduce waste. Answers like these would resonate with a green-minded company. Now would I have thought to bring this up prior to analyzing the job description? Probably not.

The self-description was followed by the "Position Overview" covering some of the broad skill packages this person should have. For example, delivering the Manufacturing Excellence (ManEx) program requires implementing the five pillars of ManEx. It then itemizes what they are. A story and/or a scripted answer that covers these bases would be wise.

Below that were more tightly detailed position responsibilities. I tend to focus on the first ones mentioned, but I look at all of them to see if they reveal patterns of emphasis, or areas where I am weak. My resume experiences will likely draw their attention to these weak spots and I need to be ready to minimize the impact of these weaknesses, or make them disappear.

A principle to remember is, "People are not looking for perfect fits, because perfect fits don't exist. They are looking for best fits." And if you can confidently speak about how your other skills can cover areas of weakness, then the issue is neutralized for the most part.

Finally, underneath this is the "Essentials" category, and this is one area where I would spend the majority of my time. If they say it is essential, then you need to prove how you exceed their expectations in these areas. Developing a story to answer behavioral questions covering each essential category is a good idea. It will make your answers seem like solutions to the problem of finding a good fit and not like a simple-sales exercise.

But what do you do if you don't have one of their essential skills, but you feel confident that this opportunity is a good fit for you? Go for it! It is amazing how "essentials" become "inessential" after you forge a positive emotional connection with the interviewer.

WHAT THEY DON'T KNOW CAN HELP YOU

I was reviewing a job description for an agency I assist, and noted how the job actually contained a large sales element. However, there was no mention of sales skills in the job description. Sometimes a job description can overlook a critical skill and, if you are the only one to recognize it, then you have gained a critical advantage.

If, for example, I was applying for this job that lacked sales skills in its description, and I had sales skills, then I would reposition the opportunity as follows:

> This business development opportunity excites me because success or failure will largely depend on one's ability to sell concepts, or the package of solutions you've developed. Selling concepts is a unique skill that many professional salespeople don't even have, but I've excelled in this arena for the last five years as my experience at Acme shows.

I have now differentiated myself from my competitors.

What makes differentiation so powerful is the emotion of fear. I've now revealed to them a key element that is needed for success in this position, and now they may fear hiring someone who does not possess it. I may have effectively disqualified every competitor, because I am the only one who can sell concepts.

I've personally used this differentiation skill in many sales situations, because it is one of the most powerful sales tools there is. I also used it when I interviewed for the previously mentioned obstetrics position—the one where I was competing with someone who was vastly more qualified than me. I told them:

> This job is not about creating a team of obstetrics monitoring experts. The obstetricians fill that role. This is about managing the launch of a new technology category, and I have done this before. It is a fairly unique skill set. It requires being able to speak passionately about a technology and generate that same passion among the early adopters....

I said it, believed what I said to be true, and I got the job. Did they really want to risk the launch of a revolutionary technology on someone who had never done this before?

Fear. It can be a powerful cause of the hiring-decision-effect. To take advantage of it, you will need to determine what your greatest strengths are that are relevant to the open opportunity. Then reposition the job in a way that favors your strengths. However, don't try this if your strengths aren't a good fit for the opportunity.

When your repositioning effort is hard to believe, then your efforts will achieve what you do not intend. The hiring authority will think you are a poor fit and, therefore, you are now unlikely to be hired.

THE ANNUAL REPORT

Annual reports can be really dry reading—unless you are Warren Buffet—but they can reveal something about the company's vision and their core values.

Where does your hiring company want to go? What are their goals? When you can show someone how your skills can help them achieve their goals, then you have tapped into the powerful emotion of hope.

Also, follow the money. What is the company investing in? This reveals their direction more than just about anything else. Is it spending a larger amount than most of its competitors on R & D, or a lot less? And is their R & D investment leading to the development of new, effective products or services? Have they just made a huge acquisition and are they struggling to integrate it into the larger company?

WHAT ABOUT YOUR NEW BOSS?

A question hiring companies expect you to ask, and you should ask, is, "Why is this position open?" This is a polite way of asking, "Did someone leave on their own after a couple of years, or were they fired?"

Why a position is open is important to you and your resume. Was the person before you terminated? If so, how long was he in this position? This could tell you if the hiring company has unrealistic expectations. Was someone only given four months to produce results?

Quick terminations might hint at a darker truth. What if the hiring authority is a trigger-happy executive, who enjoys firing people much more than coaching them? These people exist and you don't want your resume disfigured by such a person. Nor do you want to experience the toxic atmosphere they can create.

I once worked for an aging, surly president who went through four CFOs in three years. Yowza! We believed there was a trap door under the CFO's desk chair that periodically opened and deposited whoever sat there, without ceremony, on to the sidewalk.

Sometimes it helps to remember that one percent of the population are psychopaths. Their empathy system—mirror neurons—is in the off position by default. They can will themselves to feel what others feel, but they do not naturally do so. This gives them a ruthlessness that sends many to prison, and many more to high levels in organizations.

So, do your due diligence and take this issue of fit seriously. Some jobs are not worth the psychic pain and stress. And remember, when you are stressed you are functioning at half speed. You may have been a great, productive talent at every job prior to this, but if you are seriously stressed at your new job, then your results will likely be of a lesser quality.

THE GOAL OF YOUR RESEARCH

The goal of your research is to find out information that will allow you to craft answers that show how you are a perfect fit. You fit their values and have strengths that can help them advance toward the fulfillment of their vision. You will now appear to be the presenter of a solution to their problems and less of a salesperson.

Please do not look at this as a sales exercise. It is so much more. Think of it as a career fulfillment exercise, because if your research reveals how you are truly a great fit, then you will have found a fulfilling place to land.

In the following chapter we will look at how these answers can be scripted so as to achieve this goal.

15

Scripted Answers

WHY SCRIPTING ANSWERS IS SMART

I've heard this objection to scripting more times than I can count. "I think a canned answer will just make the interviewer think you aren't real. You are an actor using a script."

To which I say, "A lame answer, whether it is scripted or not, is a lame answer. A good answer, whether it is scripted or not, is a good answer. Unscripted answers have a much better chance of falling into the lame category. They will never have the clarity of a scripted answer, because they are first drafts, constructed on the fly under stressful conditions. That is hardly a recipe for success."

I will now show you what an unscripted answer can look like. The following is an attempt to answer the question, "What are your strengths?"

> I think my integrity is a great strength, because it's a quality that affects everyone and everything. It helps you build and sustain trust with others, and develop strong relationships with business partners, customers, and members on your team. Like I said, everyone. And, as a former boss of mine always used to tell me, you never know just how important integrity is until you hire

someone who doesn't have it.

[Pause, as the interviewee thinks of additional answers to this question.]

That question's always a toughie, because I think I have a lot of different strengths, but since you only asked for a few I'd have to add leadership ability. I've never had a problem getting a team to follow me and embrace the changes that I felt I needed to implement. If you were to ask my last boss what one of my biggest strengths was I'm pretty sure he'd say, "Leadership," because my team performed so well year after year.

That answer is not an interviewing crime, but it is wordy and seems to be groping toward an answer. It makes this jobseeker look a little lost and unsure of what his strengths are. He moves from integrity to the next thing that pops into his head, "Oh yeah, leadership too!"

The struggle to answer questions affects non-verbal behaviors. Instead of radiating confidence we express hesitation and doubt. We feel unsure of our answer, and the interviewer's mirror neuron system picks this up and he feels unsure about us.

When we have a scripted answer that we are confident is good, and highlights our strengths in the best possible light, then this feeling of doubt disappears. We have reason to be confident because our answer is tight, clear and well thought out.

THE SCRIPTED ANSWER

The following answer is one that comes from Jill, the transformational leader whose story highlighted how she dramatically improved the quality level at Acme. Her research uncovered the company's emphasis on a few areas that play to her strengths: quality and innovation. She can now write a script that shows how she is the solution they are seeking.

She has been asked the *what are your strengths* question after having told her story about adding $2,000,000 to the bottom line. Her answer will both address the fit issue and use repetition with variation:

> I've read articles that emphasize leadership and downplay management skills. But I think both are important, and the way I combine them is my greatest strength.
>
> As a leader at Acme, I developed a clear vision of where we needed to go, and how to get there. For example, I saw how my team needed new skills if we were ever going to innovate and produce big quality gains.
>
> Then I used some of my management tools, like delegation and coaching, to help them gain these new skills. But at first, they were a little nervous. They didn't want to fail. So, I told them, "It's okay to make mistakes. Mistakes are great teachers. They make us learn faster. But as we grow together we will begin to innovate, and that's when we'll start having fun."
>
> In a few weeks we started to develop new processes. This eventually led to a 100-fold quality improvement. It also increased our productivity and added millions to the bottom line.
>
> The last point I'd like to make is about your annual report. It had your CEO's letter to the shareholders and your vision statement. The words "innovation" and "quality" kept popping up. It seems to be a key area of focus for your company. It's also a focus of mine, because innovating makes work fun. And building a top quality product gives me a tremendous sense of pride.

In about a minute Jill has shown how she can lead and manage, delegate and coach, and produce great results. And since this company values innovators, and is seeking to hire them, Jill's answer shows she is a great fit. Achieving all of these goals with a spontaneous, unscripted answer would be difficult. Doing so without a lot of verbal clutter would almost be impossible. As Mr. Zinsser noted, "A clear sentence is no accident. Very few sentences come out right the first time, or even the third time."

The language in Jill's story is clear and concise, and it was the result of many rewrites. Her answer has a 6.1 grade level, and a 72.1 reading ease score. The unscripted answer is in the "plain English" category with a reading ease score of 60.2, but its grade level is very high, 11.1, and it is not as easy to follow.

My first attempt at writing Jill's answer was garbled and confused. I wanted to combine leadership and management skills in her answer, and I wasn't very successful. It was a first draft, so I expected this to be the case. Now imagine how much more garbled my mental first draft would be during a live job interview. I would be composing under pressure, with the possibility that my higher mental functions are now muted by the stress response.

The strengths question is a particularly important one to script. It helps us achieve the goal of articulating our strengths and associating them with results.

Since every interviewer asks many of the same questions, it helps to have scripted, edited, well-rehearsed answers to the top twenty questions or so. I will give examples of answers to a few of them.

"TELL ME ABOUT A CHALLENGE OR CONFLICT YOU'VE FACED AT WORK AND HOW YOU DEALT WITH IT?"

When faced with questions like this, think in terms of emotional impact. What situation would generate the strongest emotions in your audience, and showcase one of your greatest and most important strengths.

This is a question with a built in hook—it is asking about conflict—so pick the most engaging one you know. Here is an example:

> I think the toughest conflict situations are ones that deal with someone who has lost emotional control. Because once that happens the situation becomes completely unpredictable, and possibly even dangerous.
>
> I remember this happening to Mike. His fiancé broke off their engagement and he became a ticking time bomb. He wanted to take his anger out on somebody, and he chose our receptionist.

> I heard the loud noise he was causing and I went over there to see if there was a problem. Mike was red faced, and out of control, and the receptionist was terrified. I did not want the situation to escalate, so I approached him slowly and spoke softly. I then became the target of his anger, but I stayed calm and just kept saying, "It's okay Mike."
>
> Then I said, "Mike, let's go outside so we can have some privacy and you can tell me what has you so upset." My calmness had a calming effect. About a minute later we walked outside and the situation was defused. He later sought and received counseling.
>
> But I bring this situation up because I think it shows how I have strong communication skills. I can defuse conflict. I can handle difficult conversations. And I can keep my cool even when I am being attacked.

The power of this story is the way it can provoke a mild stress response like, "the boy is hit by a car!" You keep waiting for Mike to escalate and go postal. Such an answer will likely be remembered, as well as the candidate's coolness under fire. There are often many conflicts or challenges a person can choose from, but the best one will depict a powerful skill that produces results and is emotionally engaging. (Reading ease 69.3, grade level 6.7. An unscripted response would not approach this level of clarity.)

"WHAT IS YOUR DREAM JOB?"

This question is an attempt to discover what is perhaps the single most important criterion for hiring someone: fit. You should not immediately say, "This job is my dream job." Interviews are not forums for being cute. Instead, speak about a job in the abstract that offers similar challenges to those confronting the hiring company, and how these challenges would engage your strengths. For example:

> My dream job is working for a company that has challenges that engage my strengths. Using my strengths is what produces results for me and I enjoy using them.

For example, I'm an innovator. It is one of my strengths. And most companies face the challenge of innovating. Another strength of mine is perfecting quality processes. And again, most companies face this challenge of continually improving their quality.

[You have now brought issues of importance to the forefront of the interviewer's mind.]

The way I innovate is through the power of a team. I use my leadership skills to develop a team of innovators. Those people who are closest to the process, who deal with it everyday, tend to come up with the best ways to make the process better. I used this approach in my last two jobs and it was fun. These challenges brought out the best in me. It produced improvements in quality that were valued by my team, my company and me.

I think some of these challenges are similar to what your company focuses on, which is why I think I'm a good fit. And that is what I am seeking, an opportunity that engages my strengths and is a good fit. That's my dream job.

[Reading ease 72.8, grade level 6.1.]

I hear your objection. You can't just harp on two points with every answer. I agree. I would not develop such a mono-tonal approach. But what I am trying to illustrate is how one story—the one driving the 100-fold quality improvement—can be modified to fit the key needs that you've uncovered about a company.

"YOU ARE AT A COMPANY PARTY. WHAT WOULD YOUR CO-WORKERS SAY ABOUT YOU WHEN YOU LEFT THE ROOM?"

I never counsel clients to lie, but this question offers you the opportunity to say virtually anything and keep your integrity intact.

Here is why: No one can look into another's heart and know what he would say. Someone might praise you gushingly for reasons obscure to you, or verbally cut your head off. Since you cannot possibly know what anyone else would say, you can put almost anything into the mouths of these hypothetical co-workers and have a chance of being right. Therefore, make your answer believable by emphasizing your brand, the one you have modified slightly to fit this opportunity.

The salesperson who serviced his customer so well that they became his active, enthusiastic salespeople, might say something like this to the company that valued innovation and quality:

> I think they would say that the reason why I deliver some of the top sales results in the country is because of my out-of-the-box, innovative approach to sales. I don't just make a sale and move on. I make a sale and turn my customer into my personal sales force. I don't believe any of the other salespeople in the company are doing this. And the way I do it is through the quality of the service I offer. My customers embrace me as a colleague and a part of their team, because of the high-quality solutions my service brings them.

Note how a few tweaks modify his previous answers to questions to fit this new need for innovation and quality. Also, repeat the points you want to emphasize when answering this question, but limit their number. The one thing you don't want your answers to do is create the fog of data that tends to activate the rational mind and cause cognitive strain.

"WHY SHOULD WE HIRE YOU?"

I like to answer this one concisely and get to the point immediately. My answer would go like this:

> Fit. If I've done my research correctly, then this position is a very good fit for my strengths. I think this position requires _____ and _____ and _____. And I hope I have demonstrated that these are strengths of mine.
>
> Fit is a two-way street that needs to work for you and for me. If I am not a good fit, then neither one of us will be happy. But because I believe I am a good fit for this opportunity, I think hiring me would be a win for us both.

THE GOAL

When you answer questions clearly and concisely, and focus on the solutions you offer, you achieve the goal of complex sales: You are not selling, but you are causing the irresistible urge for them to buy.

Being armed with great answers is another source of confidence. One of the primary reasons why eighteen interviews did not intimidate Jack was because he was prepared to answer almost every question. As he wrote:

> As far as the interviewing experience, surprisingly I did have a positive experience. I felt very prepared and felt confident that I could convey my experience and skills sets in a very effective manner (clear, concise and with stories).

We rehearse a script to the point of memorizing it. This takes time and effort and many rehearsals. Even with this effort, it is unlikely you will perfectly memorize anything and that is okay. You will still remember the gist of your answers and deliver them far more clearly and concisely than if you had not rehearsed.

Then, as you demonstrate your mastery of the interviewing process by answering questions effectively and efficiently, your interviewing competence inspires the emotion of trust. Your relaxed demeanor and occasional smiles give the impression that you are comfortable, and the emotional tuning fork who is interviewing you feels comfortable as well. Fears about making a bad hire start to recede when the interviewer considers you for the job.

The funny thing about scripting answers is this: Nobody objects to scripting an answer for the question, "Would you tell me about yourself?" Almost everyone tells you to work on this answer in advance, and I am in complete agreement. But if scripting an answer in advance works for, "Tell me about yourself," then why wouldn't it work for other questions? And if not, then why not?

AVOIDING THE ONE POTENTIAL PROBLEM

A potential problem with this approach is when a person over prepares. There is a point where too much work can make you tense, and that is not the emotional state we are trying to produce. This typically becomes a problem when you try and cram in too much work at the last minute.

In the last few weeks before a marathon the runners dramatically cut back on their weekly mileage. That is because their legs need rest before the big race. Preparing for a job interview is similar to preparing for a marathon. It is a lot of hard work. But for you to perform well, you need to dial back the preparation prior to the interview.

I advise my clients to make sure they schedule in down time prior to the interview to engage in whatever it is that helps them to relax. If tea relaxes you, then find a place that serves tea and offers a relaxing environment that is close to the interviewing site. There you can camp out for an hour or so, listen to your favorite music, and take a few deep, calming breaths. Stress tends to focus the mind on problems, threats—the job interview!—and we want to relax.

I close this chapter with an attitude that needs to be avoided at all costs: A proud, superior attitude that radiates negativity. Believe it or not, it is the recommended path from one of the better-known names in the field of job search.

STUPID INTERVIEW QUESTIONS

The longer I work in this field, the more convinced I am that this maxim—always positive, always!—is becoming an irrefutable law and not just a guideline. When we are negative our tone changes in both subtle and obvious ways.

I was reading an article by Liz Ryan, the CEO and Founder of Human Workplace. She is a very influential writer on job search topics, and I had read a previous post of hers and found it excellent. I imagine the majority of her work is of this caliber, so do not think I am trying to evaluate her on the basis of one article. However, her article, *Smart Answers to Stupid Interview Questions*, does not offer sound advice.

Before she gets to the three stupid questions, and their answers, she writes the following in her Forbes article:

> Here are the three *stupidest* job-interview questions I know. If you get asked all three of them at one interview, you seriously might not want to work for this employer. They might be too in-the-box and *intellectually challenged* for you to get anything good out of the deal.
>
> If you get asked one or two of these questions, you can try a non-traditional, non-grovelly answer like the ones I've suggested below. See how the interviewer reacts. If they stop and think, or laugh, or ask you a question in return, you might be dealing with *a person who has some functioning brain cells.*[1]

Wow! As she stands in judgment from on high we now have a standard for assessing whether or not a person is *mentally challenged* or has *functioning brain cells*. If they ask these three questions, then the verdict is in: Brain damaged! I thought this was a tad negative, angry even, but I read on to see how this attitude might shape her answers to "stupid" questions.

Not surprisingly, her answers were as snarky as the previous quote.

> Stupid Interview Question: "What's your greatest weakness?"
>
> SHEEPIE ANSWER: "I'm a hard worker, and I can be too hard on myself and other people when I think that either me or somebody else could give a little more to a project."
>
> HIGH-MOJO ANSWER: "I used to obsess about my weaknesses. I used to think I had a million defects that needed correcting and I read books and took classes to try and improve them.
>
> "Gradually I learned that it makes no sense to work on things that I'm not great at, *and it makes no sense for me to think of myself as having weaknesses.* These days I focus

---

[1] http://www.forbes.com/sites/lizryan/2014/12/31/smart-answers-to-stupid-interview-questions/2/. My emphasis.

on getting better at things I'm already good at—graphic design, especially."[2]

If you don't want to get a job, then use her HIGH-MOJO ANSWER. Her answer suggests that the interviewer's question is stupid, and that is because she believes it is. She answers "it makes no sense for me to think of myself as having weaknesses." She might as well add, "And guess what, interviewer, your question is trying to make me do this." It's an insulting reply.

What is always monitoring the horizon for threats to self? It is the cognitive unconscious, aka System 1. If aroused, it can take over the interview. That is a bad outcome, because it is more emotional, instinctual and primitive. I can hear a hiring authority saying, "If you are serious about this opportunity, then you have a choice. You can pretend you don't have any weaknesses and refuse to answer my question, or you can answer the question. Which is it going to be?"

HIGH-MOJO need not answer. The interview is over.

There may be better interview questions than the ones Ms. Ryan highlighted, but treating the hiring authority as a brain-dead buffoon is not the path to job search success. Be positive in your answers to every question, even, "What kind of animal would you like to be?"

Finally, let's look at this question to see if it is truly stupid. I don't believe it is. It is a difficult question because it is unfair and, to a certain degree, unkind. You are being asked to define yourself in a negative way. It is like saying, "Please slap yourself in the face. Not like that, harder!" This does not make the question or questioner stupid. The hiring authority may ask it to see how you get out of this difficult situation.

Now imagine what might happen if you take this question seriously and answer it in a way that maximizes your strengths and minimizes your weaknesses. You will then have handled this difficult situation with mastery, not by being snarky, and this will

---

[2] https://www.linkedin.com/pulse/20140913052148-52594-smart-answers-to-stupid-interview-questions. My emphasis.

increase the distance between you and your competitors.

Always positive, always! The moment we start passing judgment on questions, declaring some to be stupid, we change our emotional relationship to the question and the person asking it. We then start to answer them in prideful ways that might make us feel good at the time, but result in rejection. We non-verbally express our contempt toward the question and toward the hiring authority for asking it. We may be unaware our contempt is so visible, but the hiring authority is aware of it and he has the stronger hand. He matches our ante with contempt of his own and raises us a rejection. We lose. Now how does that make us smart?

In the next chapter we will tackle this suicide question—"What are your greatest weaknesses?"—and others. It offers us the opportunity to shine and put more distance between the competition and us.

16

Suicide Questions

One of the most important things a company can do is hire talented people who fit, and yet most company's hiring authorities are poorly equipped to handle this task. Some are so busy with busywork that they fail to even consider what questions they will ask an interviewee until minutes before the interview.

This problem is solved by going to a website specializing in interview questions, printing the top twenty-five and—presto-chango—an interviewing god is born. Some of these top twenty-five are of the suicide variety, ones that invite you to expand upon things that can destroy your chances for success. Unfortunately, the unprepared interviewees often walk like a lemming over the edge of this cliff, as if this was their only option. However, once they understand the nature of this game, the invitations to commit suicide will go unaccepted.

Some suicide questions are:

- What are your weaknesses?
- Tell me about your worst boss?
- Tell me about your biggest failure at your last job?
- Why were you fired from your last job?

Most people hate these questions and some dread the fact that they will likely be asked them. This is a big problem, similar to hating job interviews, because it is difficult to excel at a task you despise.

Like most of you, I used to hate these questions, but after mastering them I came to love them and hoped the hiring authority asked them. What enabled me to master the art of answering suicide questions are these guidelines that take the form of a pledge:

1. I refuse to commit interviewing suicide by needlessly exposing my liabilities. I will keep them where they belong, under the surface, concealed like the mass of an iceberg.

2. When required to reveal liabilities I will reveal the barest minimum. My answers will be short and lacking in detail, because liabilities can generate negative emotions—fear, distrust, etc.—that prevent hiring decisions.

3. I will frame my liabilities with strengths, mentioning my strengths both before and after them.

4. Whenever I am requested to give a negative answer to a negative question I will respond positively. People tend to enjoy the company of positive people, and avoid the company of negative people.

5. I aim to be always positive, always!

The first question we will look at it is the oldie-goldie of the suicide question category:

"WHAT ARE YOUR WEAKNESSES?"

When asked to reveal a weakness start your answer with a strength, offer a weakness that is not job disqualifying, and then finish your answer with another strength. Or finish with an action you've taken, or process you've implemented, that shows you've mastered this weakness and are stronger as a result.

Bracketing a weakness with strengths minimizes the emotional impact of the weakness by taking advantage of the primacy and recency effects. Namely, what is said first, and what is said last, is more memorable than what is said in the middle. So we put our well-tailored liability in the forgettable middle so that our strengths are remembered and not our weaknesses.

The interviewer is asking us to violate a fundamental interviewing principle. We are always to be positive, and these liability questions ask us to do the unthinkable: Not only be negative, but be negative about ourselves. This poses a difficult challenge that we are better off conquering instead of dismissing.

SOCIAL SETTINGS

If they ask, "What are your biggest weaknesses?" then are you lying if you tell them something other than your biggest weakness?

This is an excellent question, and a difficult one to answer, but I'll try. Certain social settings require filtering information in a way that is both expected and appreciated. When you are asked at a dinner party, "How are you doing?" Do you say, "I'm in the deepest pit of hell, and I'm on a suicide watch. How are you?"

Even if this is true, you don't say it. Instead you answer, "I'm fine. How are you?"

Are you lying? Yes, because you cannot be near suicidal and feeling fine at the same time. But you lie, and aren't particularly troubled by this, because the social conventions of a dinner party demand a sunny, positive response. It's a time of entertainment, not a therapy session.

Truth is also on a holiday at funerals, and this is also expected and appreciated. At a memorial service I once heard family members praise their abusive, cold-blooded relative. It was a most uncomfortable sight, almost like the reptile sprang back to life to abuse them one last time. But they praised this departed snake because funerals are about honoring the dead, and not about sharing the unvarnished, upsetting truth.

The interview is another social setting where no one expects you to share the truth, the whole truth, and nothing but the truth, about your weaknesses. In fact, the hiring authority would be furious if everyone did. Imagine flying in four candidates for interviews and having every one of them go on at length about their many shortcomings to the point of disqualifying themselves. Is this what the hiring authority is seeking? No! They want to see how well you handle this test. This is the nature of the game, and job interviews are an important game with specific rules.

Here is what is expected of you. During an interview you are expected to present yourself in the best possible light. To do otherwise is to waste the interviewer's time and show how little you understand about this process.

The following canned, meaningless response is almost as bad as the snarky answer from the previous chapter, "I'm very decisive and sometimes make decisions too quickly."

Ugh. There are other glib variants of this response, but they all risk causing the interviewer to involuntary roll his eyeballs and stifle his gag reflex.

There is a way to answer this question so that it builds you up, and that is what we are trying to do with every answer to an interviewer's questions.

HOW TO ANSWER, "WHAT ARE YOUR WEAKNESSES?"

To answer the "weaknesses" question we sandwich it between two strengths and use an objective assessment to identify both a strength and a weakness. The answer now follows:

> I used to hate this question, but it forced me to think about my weaknesses, and do something about them. First, I didn't even know what my weaknesses were, because I'm like most people. We tend to be blind to our shortcomings. So, I turned to the Myers-Briggs Type Indicator® to get insights into my strengths and weaknesses.
>
> It told me one of my greatest strengths was the ability to take in large amounts of information, see patterns others don't see, develop creative solutions, and then have the tenacity to implement them.
>
> But it also said all types have blind spots or potential

weaknesses. According to Myers-Briggs a potential blind spot for my type can be failing to consider the impact of my decisions on the individuals in my team. And this used to happen often before I knew about this blind spot. So, to manage this weakness, I developed a leadership team from among my direct reports. They review those plans I make that will impact the entire team before they're implemented.

In almost every case this resulted in improving my plan. And, just as important, there is greater buy-in because my team knows I've listened to their input.

The beauty of this answer is that it reveals a genuine, objectively determined weakness. It also reveals a degree of emotional intelligence that the other candidates are unlikely to express in their answers to this question. This person understands that he, like everyone else, has flaws and has taken proactive steps to identify them and manage them.

Oh, and did you notice how this weakness evaporates like the morning dew when it's sandwiched between two strengths? It takes a little effort to remember this weakness and it was mentioned seconds ago. This is what you want your answer to accomplish. It should diminish or erase the negative weakness, because your goal is to be always positive, always!

The important thing is to admit a real weakness. To not do so suggests you might have an arrogance that's almost pathological. So answer this question in a way that helps your cause and not with the typical glib response, or the HIGH-MOJO answer that is disagreeable and unappealing.

"TELL ME ABOUT YOUR WORST BOSS?"

This is another question jobseekers should learn to love. Then, while you are dancing through the suicide-question-minefields your competitors have the misfortune of being hurled from one detonating mine to another.

Since we must always be positive, and limit the exposure of

liabilities, your answer to this question might be, "Thankfully, all of my bosses were great teachers who've helped me to improve. But if I were to rank order them I would say John Doe was by far my best and Joe Blow was good, but not as good."

Let's say this interviewer wants to dig deeper. Your iceberg response left a lot under cover, so he asks, "What made Joe Blow not as good?"

Because you framed your response in positive terms the interviewer will typically follow-up in like manner. We are now talking about degrees of good and not about a bad boss.

The answer starts and ends with John Doe's positive strengths:

> John Doe, my best boss, had this remarkable ability to motivate you with an encouraging word, or email, or a surprise gift from his expense account, like a gift card for having done something exceptionally well. And he would also focus on one critical detail that, if improved, would make me much better. And it did.

> Joe Blow was a kind, caring boss, but he did not have the acute observational skills that John had. Come to think of it, I've never met anyone who has developed that particular strength to that level.

Rather than wallow in a pit of human failing and negative emotion, this answer manages to turn the tables and inject positive, strengths-based excellence in its place. It presents you as someone who respects authority. It cries out: Low maintenance!

Does this positive approach create a better mood or feeling than the more direct, negative reply? Yes, and this generates cognitive ease and belief in the words you are saying.

THE STANDARD OBJECTION

Once again, the issue of truthfulness raises its noble head. Could you honestly say all of your bosses were good ones when you had a boss who was certifiably insane, abusive and immoral?

Yes, I could, and that list would include Crazy Eddie.[1]

I ever so fondly remember him taking me out on an all-night bender in Paris. I would think the evening was about to end when he would say, once again, "Let's get one more." Finally, on the elevator up to our rooms at 3 AM, he told me, "Let's have a breakfast meeting at 8 AM." There I was the next morning at 8 AM, bleary-eyed and alone at breakfast with him sleeping in.

He never had a good or encouraging word to say. He was filled with a rage that required outlets, and he believed his managers were ideal for that purpose. As for his behavior on the road, away from his wife…you don't want to know. Which explained why he was on the marriage-go-round, moving from wife to wife.

Could I call Crazy Eddie a good boss? I sure could, can, and with a clear conscience. He actually taught me some valuable business lessons that I've used at other companies. As you can imagine, such a botch of a person had to have strong business skills to offset his personal liabilities.

Would I ever want to work for Crazy Eddie again? Not in a million years. But that question is far different from whether or not he was a good boss.

Just remember that these suicide invitations are fishing expeditions. With this question the hiring authority is trying to discover if you have problems with authority. If I answer this question by gleefully stomping on the memory of a nightmarish boss, the hiring authority might think, "I wonder what he will say about me one day." Or, "It takes two to tango, so I wonder how he was a part of the problem."

Let's say a very persistent fisherman confronts you and says, "I can't believe you don't have a negative thing to say about any of your bosses. Were they all saints?"

Just smile and say, "I try to live by the rule, 'Don't say anything bad about anybody,' because even though everyone has faults, they also have strengths. I try to see the good in people, and focus on

---

[1] Even the nicknames have been changed to protect the guilty.

their strengths." If this person thinks being unable to be negative is a negative, or your unwillingness to be forced down a bad path against your will is a negative, then never hearing from this person again will be a positive outcome. These types of people, whether they are full-blown psychopaths or only have several of their traits, often specialize in making people's lives miserable and you would be wise to avoid them.

Here is another invitation to take that lemming leap:

"DESCRIBE YOUR BIGGEST CAREER-RELATED FAILURE?"

If you have experienced tremendous success over the course of your career you may want to frame your answer as follows, "That's a tough question. As my resume shows, I have overachieved my objectives every year, sometimes by a large margin. So there weren't any big failures. But I did give a really lame speech at one of our award ceremonies and my guys hounded me about it for years."

Humor can be used in interviews, particularly by someone who has made a positive emotional connection with the interviewer through stories, confident non-verbal behaviors, and demonstrating mastery over the interviewing process. When used at the appropriate time it can strengthen the emotional bond you are trying to forge.

Or, if you missed an objective one out of eight years you can answer:

> I'm proud of the fact that I made my objectives in seven out of eight years. They were all stretch objectives that were never designed to be easy. [Note: Start with a strength.]

> So, my biggest failure was missing my objective for that one year. [Note: Little is said about the weakness.]

> It was also the best thing that ever happened to my career. It led me to reconsider everything we were doing, from our training programs to our customer appreciation initiatives. And the changes we made throughout our organization resulted in me attaining my objectives every year after that.

> [Note: End with a strength.]

Again, you start with a strength, briefly state the failure, and end with a strength by transforming your failure into a positive learning experience that made you better. Or, as the once popular cliché goes, "It's all good."

The next question causes blood to drain from many faces:

"WHY WERE YOU FIRED FROM YOUR LAST JOB?"

Depending on your actual experience, you could answer in one of the following ways:

> Our company went through many downsizings and I survived all of them except this one.

> Our company was bought and during the reorganization my position was eliminated.

> There were several political factions at work and my boss headed the one that lost. He and his team were let go.

> I was the last person hired in my department and was one of many who were then let go.

> I have a history of getting along well with my bosses. They are some of my strongest references. But for whatever reason, we just could not get along. This was very unusual and I am looking forward to enjoying a good work relationship with my next boss.

The answer points to forces outside of your control, an issue that is in the past, or an exception to the rule.

Note also how the acknowledgement of a liability is short. These answers illustrate the iceberg principle. To the best of your ability, keep your liabilities beneath the surface. The only reason some of the answers in this chapter are relatively long is because they focus on strengths.

Another question that begs the foolhardy to engage in lemming-like behavior is,

"WHAT DID YOU DISLIKE ABOUT YOUR LAST JOB?"

My answer would focus on something that most people dislike. For example:

> I loved my last job. Turning my manufacturing team around was not only fun, it was rewarding. [Strength.]
>
> But the nature of my job requires maintaining lots of quality documentation, and paperwork is not my favorite task. [Liability.]
>
> However, inspectors audited this paperwork, so I always stayed on top of it. And because I did we passed every audit with flying colors. [Strength.]

Not too many people get excited about paperwork. It is a frustrating requirement of many jobs and people can relate to your disliking it because they probably dislike it as well. Even though this may be true in most cases, I still sandwich this negative between two positives.

OH NO, NOT THAT QUESTION!

Most people have one liability that makes them nervous. Every time it surfaces they freeze and their palms start to sweat. I will share what mine was—and it was a doozy—and the technique I used to overcome it.

Do you remember the story about my interviewing against someone who was far more qualified? Well, my winning out in this interview is made even more impressive by the fact that my recent job history was spottier than a litter of Dalmatians. Prior to this interview my work record showed four jobs in five years. The first company of these four was the one I left voluntarily to move back to Chicago.

I then left company number two to end my two-hour commute each way to work. It was killing me. I lived in the city of Chicago and the job was just over the border in Wisconsin.

At company number three my three years need to be measured in dog years. The CEO was the one who enjoyed eating CFOs for breakfast, then his palate expanded to include me. I refer to my termination as a mercy killing, because it was like ending a painful, terminal condition.

Finally, a friend brought me in to my next opportunity. I suppose he wanted company on what he had to have known was a bad situation. He was engaged in a power struggle, was losing, and when the company went into bankruptcy, my boss and his entire team was cut.

Boom! That was the sound of my resume exploding. So, how could I answer such an obvious, damning question in a way that was honest and capable of overcoming their concerns? I used the ARTS technique.

"A" IS FOR ACKNOWLEDGE

They asked, "You seem to have moved around a lot in the last five years. Could you tell me why?"

The first thing I said was, "I understand your concern." That's it. I've acknowledged it, but I am not going to say another word in this acknowledgement phase. I am determined to be like an iceberg, and my liabilities will remain beneath the surface. I immediately move to the next step of the ARTS process.

"R" IS FOR REDIRECT

I redirected the discussion to something in my background that showed how I was capable of loyal employment: "But I once worked for a company that lost its ability to sell its product in the U.S. due to the FDA's rescission of its 510 (k). It was on the verge of declaring bankruptcy. They cut everyone's compensation..."

The hook has been set. Now you test it.

"T" IS FOR TEST

"If I was to show you how I not only stayed with them through these personally difficult times, but also turned this situation around would that allay your fears about me changing jobs too often?"

The interviewer answered, "What happened?"

"S" IS FOR STORY

> I joined Acme, Inc., in 2000, and after being with them for six weeks an FDA inspection resulted in the rescission of our 510 (k). We could no longer market or sell our product in the U.S., and our sales in international markets were hampered by the worldwide distribution of this bad news. Hospitals from London to Beijing were aware of this rescission.
>
> The company went into survival mode. Compensation was slashed, travel expenses were cut, the CEO-founder was ousted and replaced, but even with this, our prospects for survival looked grim.

If your story has a good hook, then it draws them into the narrative and by the end of the story they are impressed by the way you've answered their concern:

> So as you can see, under the worst circumstances, and for over a three-year period, I was not one to abandon ship. Through very difficult times I remained loyal, and my actions resulted in us securing additional capital from investors. The company survived and was later sold for a quarter of a billion dollars.

Did this work? Yes, because I got the job. But let's assume it did not completely answer their concerns. That's okay because it, at a minimum, reduced their concerns. This weakness was then overshadowed by the positive energy I generated throughout the rest of this interview.

Your immediate past may generate questions that are best answered by performances further back in your career. The ARTS technique can turn a liability into an asset with a well-placed, well-written story.

All is not gloom and doom when it comes to questions. Other suicide-oriented questions allow you to use stories that can showcase your skills. One of them is,

"WHAT HAVE YOU LEARNED FROM YOUR MISTAKES?"

You could answer,

> Mistakes have been my greatest teacher. The lessons I've learned from them have helped me throughout my career.
>
> When I first became an accounting manager I had an extreme task-orientation. I focused on results to the point of forgetting there were people involved. So my style became too demanding.
>
> Fortunately I had a great boss who saw the problem and worked with me to fix it. It involved how I communicate with others more than anything else. Because of his coaching, my leadership and teambuilding skills went from being liabilities to being strengths. My rookie mistakes helped me learn some of the most valuable lessons of my career.

Whenever you can, answer questions in a way that show how you confronted a challenge and overcame it. This does two things. It engages the interviewer's interest, because conflict is interesting. It also focuses your answers on how you have grown skills that can provide solutions to problems they also might have. When you are solving problems you sell without appearing sales-y.

For example, a woman named Doris is asked, "Would your last supervisor say anything bad about you?" She turns this negative question into a positive one:

> No way! He would say something positive like, "Doris was one of the most motivated people in the company and she always led by example. It's the reason she was promoted to management."
>
> When I was working on the manufacturing line I was always on the lookout for ways to drive productivity gains by making our processes more efficient. I was always dropping ideas into our suggestion box. People made fun of me, but I shrugged it off.

Then, when they saw how I got promoted and they did not, they started to stuff the box with ideas. So I think he would say that I lead by example, and I don't let others take away my motivation. It's strong and here to stay.

In sum, liability questions, or suicide questions, deserve short, well thought out answers that reveal as little as possible about your liabilities. But when a suicide question opens the door for you to showcase your talents, then answer it with a story that shows how you overcame an obstacle, or excelled.

An area that typically receives little attention by jobseekers should be one of intense focus, because it occurs at the end of the interview. And what do people tend to remember? What is said first and what is said last.

PART 4:

FINISHING TOUCHES

17

The Interview's Endgame

CHESS CHAMPION OF THE WORLD

My father was the master of the memory-enhancing stress response. When I was growing up he would occasionally use a big word that my limited vocabulary did not possess. I would then ask him what that word meant, and he would say, "Look it up." When I tried to manipulate him into surrendering the definition he would say, "If I tell you, you will forget. If you look it up, then you will remember." And he was right.

He also applied this stress-response to the game of chess. He would challenge me to a game and would never lose. He wasn't trying to damage my self-esteem, he was simply trying to get me to elevate my game, remember my mistakes, and I did.

I wanted to change this chess-loser narrative, so I started buying books on chess. One of the most difficult and insightful books was Bobby Fischer's masterpiece, *My 60 Memorable Games*. When I bought this book, Fischer was the gifted and troubled American chess champion of the world. What I still remember about it was the way it taught me the importance of the endgame.

The endgame in chess always bored me. It often involved the advance of pawns, and the stubborn resistance against this advance from the king and a few remaining pieces. This stage was devoid of the middle game's excitement when knights, bishops, rooks and queens clashed and fell. But many of his sixty memorable games were won because of his mastery of this stage.

In the job interview you can do everything right, up to the point of the endgame, and then you can completely blow it by performing poorly in this stage. Like the endgame of chess, we may find this stage boring, or we may approach this subject last in our preparations, when we are exhausted and short on motivation. If so, may this chapter help motivate you to get up, catch a second wind, and move forward in your endgame preparations.

RESEARCH THE COMPANY

One of the purposes of researching a company is to determine if you fit their culture, the requirements of the position, and so on. For example, are they a cutthroat, take-no-prisoners type of company, and does this style suit yours? If it doesn't, then how likely is it that you will be successful at this company?

But there's another important reason why you research a company thoroughly. You must be able to answer the following question effectively, "How much research did you do on our company?" Failure to answer this question can, by itself, destroy your chances. It suggests you are a person who isn't serious about this opportunity.

Imagine being asked this question and answering, "I reviewed your Annual Report…" and before you can get any further the hiring authority says, "Great. What did it tell you? What did you find out?"

In the finest traditions of scrambling to salvage a desperate situation you might answer, "It looks like you are growing nicely."

You know your answer is weak, but you are praying the hiring authority, who is like a shark that smells blood in the water, will let you quietly swim away. Unfortunately, sharks are not known for mercy when they smell blood.

He responds, "Indeed we are, but what did you discover about our

CEO's vision for the company? Where does he want to take us?"

You are now cornered. There is no way out. So, you offer the lame truth, "I don't remember."

To which he replies, "No problem." Only, he knows it is a problem, but he is having fun and asks a follow-up question, "What else did you do for research?"

You are now his cat's paw, a toy he moves around on the floor for his amusement. He hates conducting job interviews, so he has to do something to pass the time. And since you aren't going to the next round, he feeds his ego and pride by putting your weakness on display and proving his superiority.

You may mumble a few other weak responses, but the entire time you are thinking, "No need to stick a fork in me; I'm already done."

I've experienced something similar to this during the earlier stages of my career. I've never forgotten how important it is to research a company, no matter how boring, or time-consuming the work may be. It was a lesson forever preserved by a stress-response enhanced memory.

THE HIRING AUTHORITY

Through Google, LinkedIn®, Facebook, and your own personal network, you will need to research the person who will be making the hiring decision. You want to discover potential connections you have with him.

- Where did he go to school? Was it a school similar to your own—was it a liberal arts college, or one with a great reputation in engineering?
- Where has he worked prior to this job? In what positions?
- What does he like to do in his spare time? Golf, cook, read, run?
- Has he published any articles, or appeared in any.

Then, when you first meet, you can make some small talk about a passion you both share:

> "When I was researching your company I think I read somewhere that you love to cook. Is that right?"
>
> "Wow! Your research is good. Yes, it is a passion I've had most of my adult life. Do you like to cook?"
>
> "I do. I like recipes from the Mediterranean: Italy, Morocco, Spain, Lebanon, you name it. One of my favorite websites for recipes is Epicurious. Do you use it?"

After a minute or two on this topic you can gently redirect it to the standard interview, because the mission has been accomplished. You might say, "I didn't mean to get us sidetracked on cooking, but it is fun. You probably have a lot of other questions you would like to ask."

People see what they expect to see and what they *want* to see. You are trying to make a positive emotional connection with the hiring authority, because this can make him *want* you to succeed in your interview. A conversation about a shared avocation helps make this connection. So find out whatever information you can to help make this connection stronger.

YOUR TURN

Eventually you get a chance to ask whatever questions you want. Be careful, because some questions can suggest both good and bad things about you. Good questions can show you are a person who is discriminating and interested in managing his career. Bad questions, on the other hand, can make you look like you are willing to settle for jobs that are poor fits.

So, whenever I am offered the chance to ask questions I focus on three things: The company's prospects, my fit and what they hope to find in a new hire.

The company's prospects are important, because I might be the last person hired before a downsizing. Last hired, first fired. If a company is growing, then the possibility of a downsizing is less.

So, find out what their competitive advantages are, because this has a bearing on their prospects. If they tell you, "Competitive advantage? We are the largest, most established company in this industry," then be careful. Dell, the computer maker, could have said the same thing before they tumbled. So could a host of other once-mighty companies. So check their current market share and what it was three or five years ago. Is their market share growing or declining?

I recommend asking several questions about fit, because if you don't fit, then you'll eventually quit, be fired, or be miserable. Some of the questions about fit are, "How would you characterize your management style?" "What's unique about your company's culture?" "Are there any characteristics that your star performers have in common?"

One of my final questions is, "The interviewing process typically wants to make sure the candidate is a good fit. I also want to be sure. So, now that I've covered most of my qualifications, could you tell me what the most important qualifications are for your ideal candidate?"

Some people don't want to answer this question, so I help the reluctant to get over this hump by saying, "I understand your reluctance to share this information. But it's not like I can change what I've already said. I'm just trying to find out if my strengths are a good fit." And then, of course, if you find out what they are looking for, you will pound on these points in the remaining interviews.

Another reason why I want this information is to "close" the deal. So if their answer is, "We are a results-oriented company. We are looking for someone who consistently produces and who understands how important it is to generate good results, because that's why we're paying him." I will then use this information in my final statement.

IT'S NOT, "ASK FOR THE JOB."

As I've said, the simple sales approach is all about closing. Ask for the order, or in this case, ask for the job. I've read that asking for the job is the number one thing jobseekers forget to do, and I say,

"That is good news, because asking for the job makes no sense."

The decision-making team will typically make the hiring decision behind closed doors. That is the only time you could conceivably close the deal. But guess what? Neither you, nor any of the other candidates, are in that room. So I don't try to close anyone, but I do ask to remain a part of the ongoing process.

I am convinced that this ludicrous asking-for-the-job-idea is a result of the infection caused by simple sales practices. The simple-sales emphasis is on "closing," asking for the order, and someone thought, "If this is the key to sales, then it must be the key to getting a job." Eventually a horde of unquestioning, job-search savants began to embrace and popularize this notion: We need to close this sale! We need to ask for the job!

Some coaches I respect have told me, "But expressing an interest in the opportunity is asking for the job." If that is so, then my degree in English was wasted. How does "express an interest," equate with "ask for the job"?

Here is why this discussion is important. Jobseekers are looking for guidance, and when they see the same stupidity repeated on website after website, then they begin to think they need to literally, "Ask for the job." But they can't imagine how they can do this in a way that makes any sense. That is because it doesn't make any sense.

Communication is complicated enough without saying one thing and meaning another. The sooner the job search world deep-sixes the foolish advice, "Ask for the job," the better off everyone will be. Instead of asking for the job, the following "close" to an interview is more effective.

I'd typically say something like, "You've just told me that you are looking for someone who is results-oriented. I think that's the ideal environment for me. When you look at my track record, I've consistently produced results that grew revenue and favorably impacted the bottom line. I share your results-oriented attitude, and that's why I think this is a great opportunity and a great fit for me. I'm very interested in pursuing this further, so I've got to ask, 'Is there anything you've heard that might keep me from moving on to the next step in this hiring process?' If there are any concerns, I'd like to address them."

If he says, and he usually does, "You've made a great impression on me, but once the decision-making team gets together we'll make a final slate of candidates and we will let you know, one way or the other," then I end my interview by saying:

> The last thing I'd like to say is I've done extensive research on your company, and I've found you are considered to be the best-managed, highest-quality producer of nuts and bolts in the country. You also have low turnover and high employee satisfaction, and I would be delighted to become part of your team. It was a pleasure to meet you and I hope we meet again soon.

If it is true, and everything you say should be true, then it is not false flattery to tell someone, "You work for a great company and I'd like to enter this fortunate circle." I've used this before and I've seen the hiring authority smile warmly, because I've stimulated the pride they feel about their company. When this sentiment is genuinely expressed it can be moving. People want to hire people who want the job and appreciate the opportunity. So, expressing this feeling is helpful.

THE HILL WE MUST CLIMB

There are ten or more stories, answers to anticipated questions, and answers to show how you can accomplish the job description's responsibilities. How do you remember all of this?

How you prepare makes it possible. Exercise in the morning and prepare your brain for memorizing this information. Then edit the written material several times. Read it out loud to make sure it sounds natural. Edit some more. This editing process refines your thinking, your answers, and it aids memorization. Make the sentences as easy to follow as possible. No complex sentence structures need apply. Then time them while you are rehearsing, and keep all answers below the seventy-five second threshold. By keeping them short they will be easier to memorize, and will keep the interviewer engaged as a participant in the interviewing process.

Most people will never achieve perfect recall, but that is not the goal. The goal is to provide the gist of the rehearsed answers and to keep from rambling.

Does this mean you need to work your butt off? Yes, it does. But the intense preparation pays you back the ultimate dividend. The interview is no longer intimidating. You can be relaxed and confident even if you are facing eighteen interviews in two days, for you have mastered this game.

As the great Polish pianist, I. J. Paderewski, once noted about practicing, "If I don't practice for one day, I know it; if I don't practice for two days, the critics know it; if I don't practice for three days, the audience knows it."

Even though he was a world-class talent, he still needed to rehearse daily. That said, on the day of the interview I may go over the material once and then focus on relaxing, visualizing my success, and enjoying the interview.

The preparation's tough. It's like preparing for a marathon. The twenty-mile preparation runs are never very fun. The long tempo runs can be exhausting. But if you've put in the long hours of preparation, then the day of the race is much better for you than for others. Your competitors are somewhere far behind you, cramping up and heading for a medical tent while you are crossing the finish line. Then, when you look back and see no one near you, and the job offer comes your way, the joy you will feel will last a long time.

One of the most important steps in the job search process is often overlooked: the videotaped mock interview. Few things reveal areas that require correction as much as this does. We will also look at phone interviews, one of the most difficult mediums for an interview, and one that is increasingly being used.

18

Mock Interviews and Phone Interviews

THE VALUE OF A VIDEOTAPED MOCK INTERVIEW

I'm a big proponent of rehearsing for interviews and doing this on videotape. Yes, videotaping makes this an unnatural setting, and it adds to the stress of the situation. Furthermore, a fake interview, no matter how you dress it up, is still fake. But this still does not rob the videotaped mock interview of its value.

Videotape communicates with a force that words alone lack. I can tell clients their body language is as stiff as a coiled spring. They may agree with me, but then think little of it. However, when I show them how their body language makes them look like they are ready to pounce, then the client takes the problem more seriously. There are few things more convincing than seeing your non-verbal behaviors sabotaging your chances for success.

Second, a strength of mine is an acute ability to observe and see things others miss. When I was observing salespeople and videotaping them, I was in charge of the camera, moving it back forth when someone would pace. Though this occupied my attention I would often see things in the salesperson's performance that my Region Managers would miss. They would sometimes express wonder about how I was able to do this. I mention this because my acute observational skills are not enough to catch everything. The videotape of a mock interview often reveals things I missed.

ENTER THE NON-VERBAL

I was able to observe how my client had virtually stopped breathing without watching the videotape. But this huge problem distracted me and made me miss something else. He had a habit of noisily clearing his throat, "AHEM!!!" And he did this several times.

As we watched the video, and I pointed this out to him, we could both see what a big problem this might be. In a few days he was going to be on a phone interview, and his gentle voice would bring the interviewers closer to the speaker, or they might turn up the volume, and then, "AHEM!!!"

As they grabbed their chests and quickly turned down the volume, they would realize they could no longer hear him, and so they would turn the volume back up and, "AHEM!!!"

With this one non-verbal expression of nervousness, his candidacy could easily tank. He would be the candidate generating irritation and this does not lead to job offers. But we caught this off-putting behavior in time, were able to remove it, or mute it, and he received the job offer over a favored candidate.

What made him so nervous that he was making explosive non-verbal noises and failing to breathe? Some people have stage fright. Being videotaped can make many people anxious, and that is one of the reasons why I recommend it. Training under stressful conditions prepares you for real-world stress.

GUIDELINES

Mock interviews require two people, the interviewer and you. If you are having a friend help you, who has never conducted a mock interview before, then you might want to pass these suggestions on to him or her.

Here is how I conduct a mock interview. Let's assume you are the person who is being interviewed. I will ask questions that you will probably be faced with in an interview. For example, *tell me about yourself.* Your answer to this question and others will be videotaped. Then we will watch the taped interview together.

First, I will ask you to critique your own performance by telling me what you think you did well. I will then tell you what I think you did well.

Next, you will tell me what you think you could improve on. Whatever you say you can improve on, I do not mention in my critique. That is, unless I disagree with you, and think you are being too hard on yourself.

There is a reason why I start with you critiquing yourself. First and foremost, I want to create an environment where criticism is safe and accepted. It's easier to hear criticism from your own mouth than from others. That's why you go first, and also why I don't repeat your accurate criticisms. If you know what needs to be fixed, then why do I need to repeat it? I merely note that I agree with you on those points.

When you are finished critiquing yourself, I will then tell you what else you can do better. I typically focus on one behavior that requires changing. To change one behavior is difficult enough, but going after three or four simultaneously is virtually impossible. However, when we focus on one there is a greater likelihood that a bad behavior can be deleted, or a new success-behavior can be added to the interviewee's repertoire.

After the critique, you will rehearse what needs improving. I'll be watching and giving you feedback as needed. Once you feel good about it I will videotape you again and then we will again critique this performance together to see if you've improved, or if another session is required. If it still needs improvement, we will wait at least a day before trying again.

WHAT YOU CAN DO

You might wonder how you can put this information to use. You don't have a video camera, and finding someone who does, and will tape you, might be difficult. That said, there are still viable options for you.

If you have a smart phone, then buy a simple tripod for it, prop it up on a desk, sit in front of it and push the video record button and have a friend ask you questions. Once you've recorded the mock interview, transfer it to your Mac or PC and, with your friend watching it with you, replay it.

You get to be the first one to critique yourself, and the first thing you mention are all of the things that you did well. Your friend should try to note other things you've done well. Noting the things that require improvement follows this. Are the non-verbal behaviors strong, or do they need work? Is there a common problem in the way you answer most of your questions? Are you rambling, unclear, or lacking in positive, confident energy? Next, your friend offers his critique.

Encourage their honesty and listen to the criticism instead of reacting to it. Their assessment is vital. They are more objective about you than you can ever be, so the last thing you will want to do is angrily disagree with them.

Obviously this set up is not as effective as being critiqued by a trained observer. You will likely miss some things. But it will catch the big mistakes that might have disqualified you from advancing in the interviewing process.

PHONE INTERVIEW NOT PHONE CALL

Unless you love to talk on a telephone, phone interviews are no fun. They are like Ms. Cuddy's stone-faced, emotionless interviewer who gave no emotional feedback to the person he was interviewing. This is because the phone removes all non-verbal feedback except for tone of voice, and it negatively affects a person's tone as well. Phones do a poor job of capturing the undertones and overtones that give a voice its richness. Phones make what is already difficult even more so.

I am not a huge fan of phone interviews, but I understand why they are growing in popularity. They are a quick, inexpensive screening device, and they appear to be the new first step in many job interviews. Therefore, we must gain a greater affection for this medium by mastering it.

The following mindset helped me embrace phone interviewing: I never viewed a phone interview as a phone call. It was simply a job interview that required me to adjust my style.

PREPARING FOR A PHONE INTERVIEW

We prepare for phone interviews virtually the same way we would for a regular interview. We research the company, the job description, and the interviewer.

A phone interview is typically shorter, lasting only twenty to thirty minutes. They are like quick scans of a resume. If there are glaring errors, then that resume is shoved aside. And if someone on a phone interview is unclear, or drones on forever, then they get excluded as well. However, I have known phone interviews to go on for forty-five to sixty minutes and be followed by a hiring decision.

The shorter interviews may seem like they last forever, but stress can warp our perception of time. Because they tend to be short, don't save your best stuff for last, or you may never get a chance to share it. Your research should uncover two or three critical skills a person in this position must have. Have a brief story for each one of them.

The seventy-five second rule does not apply to the phone interview. I would apply the minute-or-less rule. Answers need to be shorter because the medium does not play well with long responses.

As with every other aspect of interviewing, style is crucial. They have to see you through your voice. So listen to how you sound over the phone. Call your own phone number and leave yourself a voice mail that gives an answer to an interview question. Be sure to use a phone recording, because it will approximate the way you sound while speaking over the phone.

Ask yourself, "How does my voice make me look? Do I sound

tired or energetic, distant or warm?" In other words, what emotions are evoked by my voice?

If your voice sounds flat, then practice talking with a smile. Many people have used this technique to give their voice warmth.

I also recommend turning off call waiting. Every phone system may be unique, but here is how I do it when I am being interviewed on the radio. When the producer calls, about 2 minutes before I go on the air, I ask, "Would you mind staying on the line for about ten seconds while I switch off my call-waiting?" They happily oblige and I then press: flash, * 70, flash, flash.

In your case, I would say to the interviewer, "Before we get started, if you like, I can turn off the call waiting. It takes about 5-10 seconds." He might say, "No need to worry about that. The last person who tried that ended up hanging up the phone on me, and I don't want a possible repeat. So, let's get started." If they are okay with possibly being interrupted with beeps during the call, then that is their prerogative. But if they want you to disable the call waiting, be sure this is something you have practiced.

BREATHING

I highly recommend having notes in front of you, so long as you don't have to noisily shuffle paper, or change your posture in a way that negatively impacts your tone of voice. For example, when you are looking down to read notes you can affect how deeply you breathe. This can affect the richness of our tone that depends on air.

Try this experiment using a high-fidelity recording device—smart phone tape recorders work well, but a microphone into a Mac using Garage Band works better. It also gives you a voiceprint that gives you visual feedback.

Record your voice as you read a few of your favorite sentences from a book. In the first recording retract your stomach muscles so that you cannot breathe deeply, then breathe into your chest and read the sentences out loud while recording them.

Next, breathe deeply into your abdomen. Your stomach should

distend. Then record your voice as you read out loud the same sentences. Finally, replay the recordings one after the other, and see if you can hear the difference. Abdominal, or diaphragmatic, breathing can give your voice a richness that it does not now have, unless you currently breathe this way. This will help you in phone interviews, face-to-face interviews, and life itself.

Standing while speaking can make diaphragmatic breathing easier, and this not only makes your voice richer, it tends to give your voice more energy. Try it out. Record it and see if it works for you.

ADDITIONAL POINTS

Along with your notes, a copy of your resume is a good idea. If they refer to it, seeing it might help you formulate a better answer.

Soundproof your interview. No music or TV in the background, and no dogs or cats in the room.

Have a glass of water nearby in case your nerves give you dry mouth.

And, as with all interviews, be prepared to ask questions. I'd particularly key in on *fit* questions, management style, and culture.

To communicate your interest in this opportunity you can end the interview with this question: "Based on the job description, my background, the company's culture and your management style, I think I'm a great fit for this position and that makes this opportunity very interesting. So I guess my final question is, is there anything preventing me from moving onto the next step in this process?"

If they say, "I have no concerns," you can add, "Great. What's the next step?"

He might then say, "A final slate of candidates will be drawn up this afternoon and we will contact those candidates tomorrow."

I would conclude by saying, "I hope to hear from you tomorrow and I've enjoyed speaking with you."

NEXT STEPS

You are now ready to conduct the formal job interview. Congratulations! It took a lot of hard work to get here. In the next two chapters we will explore ways of connecting you with hiring authorities who just may have the job you seek.

19

Networking Through Informational Interviews

INFORMATIONAL INTERVIEWS

Informational interviews are an excellent way to tap into the hidden job market, the opportunities that never get posted. Many people are intimidated by informational interviewing, because they have yet to regain their confidence and they feel they are bothering people, or because they don't understand how this process unfolds. This chapter will begin by covering a structured approach that makes informational interviewing both effective and easier. Then it will address the confidence issue, and the winning attitude jobseekers must adopt.

The first step is developing a list of all of your networking contacts: Friends, colleagues from prior jobs, contacts from alumni and professional associations, people you know from church or other organizations, in other words, everybody.

Your goal is to get three new contacts from each of these initial contacts. Do these people know anyone who is currently working and is a hiring authority? Those are the important contacts, as are people who have extensive networks. And don't forget; when someone shares a new contact with you always ask him if you can reference his name. It can keep you from ending up in your new contact's spam folder.

TARGETED INDUSTRIES

The purpose of an informational interview is, in part, to get information from someone in a specific industry, to see if they think your skills are transferrable to their world. Certain industries are better fits for your skills, or are more interesting to you. Whatever industries you decide to target, limit their number to three.

The reason why we limit the number of industries you target is to take advantage of the *small world* effect. People know people within these industrial small worlds, and your networking within a few industries improves your chances of being noticed within them. When you go after every industry at once it is harder to become a known quantity, or generate buzz about your candidacy.

You will start by making a list of companies in your targeted industries. Then you will research them to develop a list of hiring authorities, their contact information, and whatever personal information you can find.

WARM CALLS

This is the point where many people balk at informational interviewing. They reason, "I won't know these people, and they won't know me. I don't want to cold call people I don't know. Why would they want to waste their time with someone who calls them from out of the blue?"

This is very reasonable, and I agree with this argument. Cold calls have an extremely high failure rate. Therefore, we need to warm these calls up. These warmth-generators come from research you will conduct on Google and LinkedIn® on the people you want to meet. And by warm call, I do not mean a phone call. Usually your first contact will be by email. These emails, however, also need to be warmed up.

Let's say you want to meet Jane Doe. It could be Jane was just mentioned in a business article a few months ago. By referencing this article in your initial email you warm the email up.

If you have any personal connection to Jane, this warms up the email. Did she once work in the same industry as you? Did she attend the same school, or a school in the same state? Does she have the same major? Is she a member of one of your professional organizations? Did someone, anyone who knows her, refer you to her? By mentioning these tenuous connections the email goes from cold to warm.

We'll cover what you would say in just a moment, but what is easy to forget is this: There is a hidden job market. The person I am speaking to may not have a position open for me, but he may know of someone in his industry who is looking. Or you may so wow him that he thinks, "We've always needed someone with these skills. Let's create a position."

Let's return to eighteen-interview Jack. The reason why his informational interview suddenly became a job interview was because he had stumbled upon two unposted, unadvertised job opportunities that had just become available—in Atlanta and Tampa. He became the first outside person to know about them because he was trying to conduct an informational interview.

There are other benefits gained from informational interviews. You get experience interviewing; you may learn of new ways to employ your skills that you never imagined; and you can expand your list of contacts.

PHASES

The first phase of the campaign involves you talking to anyone and everyone. The next phase may involve you speaking with people in targeted industries who occupy a job-level similar to your own, or who are one to two levels higher than you. Ultimately, you want to spend time with those who work at a level higher than yours, but your peer-group can offer valuable information. Since you are seeking a job that is either the same as theirs, or similar, they can help clarify whether or not your skill-sets fit the requirements of the job, and the ways in which they do.

SECURING THE INTERVIEW

To secure the informational interview I recommend going through these steps:

1. Send an email or a message to your targeted contact through LinkedIn®.
2. The email will mention a future phone call to arrange for an informational interviewing date and time.
3. Call and secure the interviewing time slot.
4. Conduct the interview.
5. Write to express your thanks and gratitude.
6. Update them on your progress.

We keep them updated for several reasons, some obvious, some not. First, we do it out of a sense of professional courtesy. If they have extended to us the gift of their time to help us down the path, then we should update them whenever we make progress. The note needs to be short, positive and pleasant. This serves another purpose and that is keeping our name at the forefront of their mind. When they do find out about a new opportunity we don't want to be the people they've forgotten about.

THE INITIAL CONTACT BY EMAIL

Reaching out to someone who doesn't know you can be tricky, but the following start to your email makes it less so:

> Hi Joseph,
>
> My name is Tom Payne and I received your name from Edward X, your counterpart at Acme, Inc. In managing my career transition, he recommended you as a helpful contact. I'll begin by telling you a little bit about myself, and then my reason for contacting you.

You mention the referring person's name at the beginning of the email, and also in the subject line. It could read, *Subject: Referral from Edward X.*

BRANDING STATEMENT

The next paragraph is an abbreviated branding statement. It gives a brief overview of an achievement and your skill sets. Brevity is critical. You don't want hiring authorities to look at a lengthy email and delete it because they don't have the time or inclination to read a treatise.

The email should be able to fit on a single page (with normal margins, etc.), and the branding statement should take up the bulk of your message. Its purpose is to show your warm-call contact how you are someone worth knowing.

One difference to this branding statement from others is the way you will want to make it broader in its appeal. You will be speaking to people in industries different than yours. So you will want to speak about how your achievements demonstrate problem solving, teamwork, and other abilities that apply across businesses.

The following is an abbreviated version of the salesperson who appeared in "The Branding Statement" chapter:

> I am in sales and the way I consistently deliver results that rank me in our company's top five salespeople is by turning my customers into my personal salesforce.
>
> I do this by taking the time to customize solutions for them that generate deep satisfaction. It makes them feel like I am a part of their team, because I am. Then, when I bring prospective customers to these accounts, they sell the prospect on my company, our solution and me. That is how I won the business of Acme, Inc., currently our company's largest account.

In less than thirty seconds I've become someone who is worth knowing.

REQUEST

The third and final paragraph requests the informational interview.

> To advance my career, I am looking to employ my talents in your industry. To help make this transition I would like to benefit from your perspective through a brief, twenty-minute informational interview. To arrange a time I will call your office next week. I thank you in advance for your consideration.

The tone exudes the confidence of a person who is a solution seeking a hiring authority's problems. Also note, in less than 200 words, taking up not even half a sheet of business stationery, I've communicated why I am contacting the person, who I am and what I hope to achieve. A concise message does not require much of their precious time.

THE INTERVIEW

When I tell people that Marty Gahbauer conducted over 100 informational interviews their initial response is something like: And does Marty compete in 100-mile ultra-marathons? To my knowledge, he does not. But superhuman strength and determination are not necessary, because this informational interviewing process can actually be fun.

Perfect strangers know what it's like to be out of work. Most will want to help, particularly if you present yourself in a confident and interesting light. In some ways I found this process restored some of my shaken faith in humanity. It was encouraging to receive help from complete strangers. Like so much else in life, the task is far more enjoyable once you've broken the code.

You've secured the interview, arrived at their office in your appropriate attire, and are armed with your best questions. After engaging in some preliminary small talk, your opening might sound like this:

> Thanks again for your time. I'd like to start by offering a brief summary of some of my strengths, because they are directly tied to the questions I will be asking.

> As I mentioned in my email, I am a consistent, top-producer in sales....

Remember, repetition with variation is your friend. It creates the condition of cognitive ease that biases the mind toward belief. And you need to restate your value because of the questions that will follow. These questions will try to unearth problems that your skill sets can solve, because you are a solution seeking a hiring authority's problems. With the branding statement delivered, you now ask:

> Are my skills a good fit for organizations in your industry?
>
> What positions within this industry are the best fits for me?
>
> In those positions, what are the most important skills that a person should have to be successful?
>
> How often do companies like yours hire from outside of the industry?[1]

What am I trying to accomplish with these questions? I'm trying to get this person to see me employed in their industry. I've given them a portrait of my value, and now I am asking them to imagine my skill sets thriving in their field. If I do this effectively enough, then several good outcomes can occur:

- The best outcome: They offer me a job. (Yes, the informational interview is not a job interview. You do not go in and immediately hand someone your resume. But that does not mean it cannot turn into a job interview.)

- An excellent outcome: They refer you to someone who is trying to fill a job that would fit your skills.

- A very good outcome: They call their hiring-authority contacts and tell them about you, give you their contact information, and let you use their name to establish contact.

The goal is to illustrate the way you would provide organizations

---

[1] Online you can find resources offering 200 informational interviewing questions, and you can pick and choose them according to what you think works best.

like his significant value, because this increases the likelihood he will give you some of his contacts. When you make a favorable impression on someone they want to share your name with others. You are a good catch and they want their friends to enjoy the benefits you offer.

To achieve this goal of gaining their contacts you ask the following at the end of the interview, "Do you know of anyone in your industry that I should contact to continue this transition process?"

Whether he gives you additional contacts or not, thank him and ask one last question, "Is there any way I can help you?"

There are a couple of reasons why you offer your help, but first and foremost it is good to give and you have a lot to offer. From a purely psychological standpoint, it builds you up. You are not approaching people like a beggar waiting for a hand out. You are a professional whose skills can help an organization and a hiring authority, and you offer to help them whether they reciprocate or not. It could be that your kindness leads them to reciprocate by being helpful to you.

MISCELLANEOUS NOTES

As mentioned above, you do not offer or leave your resume unless they ask for it. The informational interview is not a pretext to conduct a job interview, or turn it into one. You've said this would be an informational interview, so it needs to remain one. But always carry a resume with you, because if they ask, "Did you bring a copy of your resume?" you can answer, "Yes. I always carry one in my briefcase, because you just never know when someone might ask for one."

If the interviewer loves you and keeps talking, and the interview goes over twenty minutes, that is okay. A good rule of thumb is: Most people schedule their work in 30-minute blocks. This means that once the interview starts to go over 30 minutes you should thank them for their time and offer to terminate the interview. However, there are always exceptions to every rule. Therefore, if this person is very insistent about keeping you there to learn more, then oblige him.[2]

YOU ARE NOT A PROBLEM SEEKING A SOLUTION

Before you go out and meet people, you need to radiate confidence. This ability is helped by the five techniques I detailed to help you control your emotional state. Taking control of your attitude toward your situation and yourself is the sixth technique.

I see different degrees of the following self-defeated attitude in almost every client. They believe they are a problem seeking a solution, an unemployed person seeking a job. They define themselves by what they lack—their joblessness—and this attitude infects the entire job search process, particularly the ability to network successfully.

One of my clients once said, "I'm going to a party this weekend and our Alderman is going to be there.[3] I'm guessing he has more local business contacts than just about anybody. Do you think I should network with him to see if he has any opportunities?"

Before I could speak he continued, "I guess that would be a bad idea. After all, it's a party. He probably wouldn't want to be bothered." And I thought, "Not as long as you have that attitude."

He viewed himself as a problem seeking a solution and one could argue, "But that is reality. After all, he is unemployed and he is seeking a job."

This is true, but the following is equally true. He was also a solution to a hiring authority's problems. He had skills and abilities that could address a company's needs, but he failed to look at his

---

[2] Much of this material on informational interviewing comes from executive outplacement training I once received. It corresponds with information shared by Martin Gahbauer at the Career Transitions Center of Chicago. My interview of Marty can be downloaded for free at www.tompayne.com/podcasts.html.

[3] Alderman, in this instance, is a Chicago city government position. Chicago is divided into fifty legislative districts, or wards, and an Alderman is an elected official who represents a district. They are members of the Chicago City Council.

pluses, because the negative hypnotized him. The invisible assassin—his poisoned attitude—was destroying his job search chances, and he needed to slay this assassin by dramatically changing his attitude.

By changing his attitude he could go from being a negative, life-force-sucking, energy drain that people avoided, to being a positive, life-enhancing, mood-elevating personality that people enjoyed being around.

So, repeat after me, "I am a solution seeking a hiring authority's problems." Once you believe this statement that is objectively true, you will have made dramatic progress on the path to job search success.

Had my client believed this he could have gone up to the Alderman and said:

> Bill, based on what you've said, your goal seems to be to bring value to your constituents and I think I can help. I specialize in turning dysfunctional teams into high-performance teams. The last team I worked with added $2 million to the bottom line. I'd like to schedule a twenty-minute meeting with you to discuss who my skills might be able to help. Who should I call to set up a meeting?

Would this work? It is impossible to say since this scenario is hypothetical, but this much can be asserted: This positive approach offers the possibility of success, while the negative, hopeless approach offers none.

APPLYING THIS IN THE REAL WORLD

Jobseekers are not the only ones crippled by this "I am a problem seeking a solution" attitude. I was coaching a client who was finding some aspects of her job difficult. She was a researcher who analyzed an industry, like food, and her job required producing reports on the trends in her specific industry. These reports required her to contact people working in this industry and interview them. Ideally she should have ten interviews per report, but she struggled to produce five.

I asked her what was causing the problem. She gave a list of excuses that were pretty lame, so I asked her, "You don't seem to like this part of your job. Why?" The real problem soon surfaced.

She replied, "I feel like I am bothering people. I don't like people to bother me, and I don't like to bother other people."

She was a problem, seeking a solution. So, I told her, "Your attitude is way off base. These companies need to speak with you. You offer them the opportunity of giving their perspective about their products. And aren't your reports read by people around the world?"

"Yes."

"So, the next time you call them you say, "Hi, my name is ____, and I work for _____. We publish reports on your industry that are circulated throughout the world, and wanted to give you the opportunity to tell us about your products. This discussion will provide us with insights, but oftentimes the food companies we interview receive insights as well. When might we schedule an interview?"

It took some time to convince her that she was a solution to their problems, but this attitude took root. The next time I saw her she had scheduled ten interviews, and one of them involved a personal invitation to visit the company at their office. She was now a solution, a positive force, and this attitude change meant the difference between failure and success.

TECHNOLOGY

We live in a world that is rapidly changing and this impacts some aspects of job search. Two of the more important changes are the emergence and use of videoconference interviews via Skype, and social media networks like LinkedIn® and Twitter. In the next chapter we will look at ways to take make sure your style accommodates these technological innovations.

20

Technological Twists

With the ever-increasing speed of change, what keeps this material from being dated? For example, algorithms now process millions of resumes daily, and the way the algorithms are designed keeps changing. This requires an ever-evolving approach to resume writing. So, how can this material be relevant a year from now?

To these concerns I say, "A chapter on resumes is conspicuously absent from this book for that reason. And what I will cover about LinkedIn®, and other technologies, may soon be out of date. But most everything else is based on human nature. When Gutenberg invented the printing press in the fifteenth century, human nature didn't change. When the Internet came on line, human nature didn't change. And when we decoded the human genome, guess what? Yep. Human nature didn't change.

But technology does introduce some interesting twists to the job search process that need to be addressed. Since style is still more important than substance, technology does confront us with some new style considerations.

LINKEDIN®

Finding a job is all about networking and LinkedIn® is one of the most important job-related networks. It is a must for jobseekers. Recruiters, small businesses and large companies use LinkedIn® to find employees. There are many ways to take advantage of this tool, and a few of them follow.[1]

THE PROFESSIONAL HEADLINE

The "professional headline" for LinkedIn® appears right below your name. It shouldn't be your current job title. Instead use this important piece of web real estate to tell everyone what it is you do and to employ key words that help you turn up in searches.

As soon as you start editing the headline a box will appear that you can type your new headline into. Beneath this is a line that says: "See what other users in your industry are using." By clicking on this you can get ideas about the right keywords you need to use. Also, an attention-getting statement helps.

You have 120 characters to play with in this headline and I recommend employing as many of these characters as possible. My headline is *Management Consultant, Author, Speaker: Improving Sales/Communication/Teams/Job Search Through Neuroscience and Coaching*. That covers a lot of ground and uses up all 120 characters. It also has a lot more punch than simply saying, Management Consultant.

Keywords can also be sprinkled throughout the sections in your profile, to include: Current Job Title, Summary, Additional Job Titles, and Skills.

Think of keywords like a Chicagoan thinks of voting. In Chicago people believe in voting early and often, and we need to use keywords the same way. Let them appear early in your profile and throughout it, but not to the degree that your profile becomes

---

[1] Books are written on this subject so I cannot cover the many tips and tricks about LinkedIn® in one chapter. Therefore, I recommend you consider buying one of the many books on this subject. The reference I've used for this chapter is Brenda Bernstein's, *How to Write a Killer LinkedIn® Profile: And 18 Mistakes to Avoid*. It is chock full of good advice that she continually updates (she is on the 11th edition).

unreadable.

The job title field benefits from this approach:

> You have 100 characters to play with, so use them! Here are some examples of job titles that are keyword optimized:
>
> ### Example # 1: Senior Legal Manager/Counsel
>
> Senior Legal Manager: EMEA > Trusted Legal Counsel | International Deals | Compliance
>
> ...According to BrandYourself, LinkedIn® is the social network that most often appears at the top of Google search results, ranking "higher than all other profiles including all other social networks and website builders."[2]

Our goal is to be the person a recruiter or hiring authority finds. If keywords help your LinkedIn® profile appear at the top of Google searches, then you are well on our way to being contacted.

CONTACT INFO

When you click on the "Contact Info" box, beneath your Education and number of Connections, you will see that certain information like your phone number is only available to your contacts, while information you may have entered about your website, or websites, is available for all to see. It can look like this:

> Websites Company Website
>   Company Website
>   Company Website

In other words, these different pages are indistinguishable from one another. But when you are editing this contact information you can choose "Other" instead of "Company Website." When you do this, another box will appear and I entered the following information into it: TomPayne.com Homepage. By clicking on this link you would be taken to the home page of my website. I also customized the other two boxes so that people could click on links

---

[2] Brenda Bernstein, *How to Write a Killer LinkedIn^R Profile: And 18 Mistakes to Avoid* (eBook, 2014), location 274-275.

to access my blog, or the consulting services section of my website. This LinkedIn® "Websites" section now looks like this:

>Websites TomPayne.com Homepage
>Tom Payne's Blog
>Consulting Services

This makes this section intelligible and it might lead someone to explore your profile further.

PUBLIC PROFILE URL

The other area that is stylistically challenged is the gobbledygook URL that LinkedIn® generates and displays to the left of your contact info. The way to change it into something meaningful, and relevant to your brand, is to hover your cursor over your public profile URL and then click on the editing icon. A page will open and on the top right of the page there will be a link entitled "+ Create your custom URL." When you click on the link you can then fill in the space after, "www.linkedin.com/in/_____."

Since my name, Tom Payne, is fairly common it was long gone by the time I learned of this trick. LinkedIn® let me know this by telling me "tompayne" was taken, but offered "tompayne5," and several other options. I ended up choosing "tompayneconsulting," which was also available.

Where this modification might come in handy is on a business card that notes your LinkedIn® public-profile URL, or on correspondence. It is much easier to type in "tompayneconsulting" than a random string of numbers and letters.

THE SUMMARY

The "Summary" section is easily overlooked, or is treated like the "Summary of Qualifications" section at the top of many resumes. The Summary should sum up your strengths, the value you offer, and connect it with accomplishments. It is like the branding statement in that regard, but because it is part of an online network that is scoured by search algorithms, it is also an ideal spot for placing keywords.

To achieve both ends, I began this section with my brand.

> I am a management consultant who helps clients align business practices with human nature—i.e., the way we process information, make decisions, form habits, and so on. This is achieving the difficult goal of changing an organization's behavior both in the U.S. and overseas in areas as diverse as creative problem solving, team building, communication, leadership and sales.

I then followed it with results this approach produced:

> This system produces results. By realigning sales practices to produce the emotions that cause the buying-decision-effect, a small, unknown Midwestern company grew to >50% market share selling multi-million $ digital data and voice communication systems to hospitals while competing against multi-billion $ rivals (GE, Tyco, Hill-Rom).

I offer the endorsement of this system from an immensely influential expert.

> This sales system was detailed in my book, *The Causes of Sales Success*, that was favorably reviewed by Neil Rackham, a leading sales authority and the NY Times bestselling author of *Spin Selling*.

And then I show how all of this was adapted to serve jobseekers, a group I feel committed to serve.

> These complex sales skills were then adapted to help jobseekers interview more effectively and my public speaking on this subject is reviewed below in "Projects."

I then close this section with a listing of international assignments that enable me to repeat keywords several times:

> International Assignments Include:
>
> Training diverse groups of European Salespeople in Rome, Frankfurt and Bonn on: The art of differentiation, the creation and use of stories, communication—mastering non-verbal communication and developing a powerful leadership voice that persuades—how to make

presentations more visual and effective, team building, creative problem solving, determining individual strengths and leveraging them, how to develop powerful phrases and why repetition can be so effective.

Training of these salespeople involved return assignments. The attendees requested these additional courses.

THE GOLDEN RULE

Be giving. Do to others what you would have them do to you. Write unsolicited recommendations of others, because LinkedIn® will then ask them if they want to return the favor. It is an effective way of gathering additional recommendations. If this fails to generate recommendations, then ask people you know if they will write one. And, to make it as easy as possible, provide them with a copy of what you want them to say.

LinkedIn® is a unique world and when we arrive in a new world it helps to have someone who has spent time there to serve as our guide. There are too many customs, guidelines, tips and whatnot, regarding LinkedIn®, for me to share in this small space. So, I recommend researching the available how-to-use LinkedIn® guides, buying one and following it.

VIDEOCONFERENCING INTERVIEWS

In an Office Team survey HR Managers were asked, "How often, if at all, does your company conduct job interviews using video technology?"

In 2011 that question was answered, "Very Often" only one percent of the time. In 2012 that percentage skyrocketed up to fifty-three percent! This is a technological twist that appears to be here to stay, that is, until it is replaced by a new technology.

To prepare for a Skype interview, practice conducting one with a friend over Skype on the same computer, and from the same location that you will be using during your interview. This will get you comfortable with the format, and it will allow your friend to check out the lighting, your outfit, appearance and so on.

Some things that you can't see will be obvious to someone else. For example:

- I can barely see your eyes because of the way the lighting casts shadows.
- Or your forehead looks so bright and shiny it is distracting. (Guys, unless you appear on television, then you may not know about the value of applying powder to your face. Ask a female friend, or your wife, if you need help with this step.)
- The color of your blouse is too loud and distracting, as is its pattern. Solid colors are better options.
- The background shouldn't be a large painting, because all I want to do is look at the painting.
- Don't multi-task during this interview.
- No dog in the room. You don't want the interviewer to be jolted into another dimension by an unexpected, loud bark.
- Keep it out of the way, but a glass of water may come in handy if you develop a case of dry mouth.
- Keep a piece of paper and a pen nearby for taking notes.
- The great thing about Skype is it allows you to have post-it notes all over your computer to remind you about stories to tell and to smile. Please smile. A Skype interview is unnatural at first, and when we experience new things that are stressful we tend to be dead serious, emphasis on dead.

TWESUMES

A twesume is a 140-character, condensed, resume that can be broadcast on Twitter. They are designed to take advantage of a trend in corporate America. Companies are posting job opportunities via Twitter with links to take you to their career site. Twesumes do something similar by providing links to the jobseeker's resume, website and so on.

Start by composing your twesume. Include in it: What you do, an accomplishment, a skill-set, your goal and a link to a more detailed profile. You can also add the hashtag: #twesume. You then tweet this twesume to your followers, direct message it to companies you are interested in, and even use this as your Twitter bio.

It doesn't seem like it will take a lot of work, but never underestimate the difficulty of making 140 characters powerful enough to generate a response.

Jobvite conducted its Social Recruiting survey in 2012 and found:

- 92% of recruiters use social media as a part of their recruiting strategy.
- The top social networks used for recruiting were LinkedIn® (93%), Facebook (66%) and Twitter (54%).
- After the big three, the percentage drops dramatically: Blog (21%), Google+ (20%), YouTube (19%).

With so many recruiters using social media, it makes sense to pay attention to these tools, and Twitter may be the tool jobseekers use the least.

All of this technology-related stuff can get out-of-date quickly. Not too long ago LinkedIn® was a small boutique app used by few. Now it's a mainstream app used by hundreds of millions. So, research the web to find out what new tech trends in job search are now important.

THE JOB SEARCH CAMPAIGN

Companies want people who can think outside of the box. So, creative people are launching job search campaigns that include developing their brand on a website.

These websites can have videos of the candidate, videos of people giving testimonials about their impact, and marketing campaigns that differentiate their product—themselves—from other candidates. You could post an interactive resume on this website with links to your blog, or to a position paper on teambuilding, or other important topics related to your field.

One of the skills in the resume might be a link to a videotaped answer. For example, click on *problem solving* and the person with a job opportunity might be taken to a YouTube video that shows you telling a story about a problem you faced in a work situation and the way you solved it.

There are endless ways to be creative about a job-search campaign, and this could open doors for you that would otherwise have remained closed.

In the next chapter we will cover one of job search's most emotional stages: negotiation. Because of the emotional intensity of this stage, it is a phase where costly mistakes are often made.

21

Negotiation

You put in a tremendous amount of work, and you worked smart. None of your competitors did the same. And even though you may have entered this contest in last place in the eyes of the interviewers, you quickly vaulted to first place during the interview and you got the job offer. Congratulations!

Prior to receiving the phone call from the hiring company that extends the offer, get mentally and emotionally ready. This is a critical time where many jobseekers stumble. First, you thank whoever is calling and express genuine excitement about the opportunity. Then ask them for a week, or five business days, to think about the offer.

If they wonder why you need so much time, and ask if something is wrong, just say, "Oh no. Nothing's wrong. It's just that this decision is so important. It could literally change the course of my career. So I just need some time to get over my excitement, talk to friends and family, think deeply about what you've offered me, and come up with an appropriate response. And that takes time."

The HR person is usually good with that and will mark their calendar and await your response.

The request for extra time accomplishes several things, but

foremost among them may be this: With each passing day all of the other candidates become less viable choices should you have difficulty coming to an agreement. This strengthens your negotiating position.

When you interview well you will generate what is almost like a yearning for you to become a part of the hiring authority's team. This yearning produces strong offers, so don't be shocked if you get one. It might seem to be almost embarrassingly good. It can make you feel uncomfortable about asking for more. If that is the case for you, then I have three words of advice: Get over it.

As a friend of mine once told me, "You can love your wife and you can love your dog, but it's not real smart to love your job, because it can't love you back." What he was trying to say was, "It's business." So don't let your great change in fortune rattle you.

Some people worry, "If I ask for more, doesn't that run the risk of angering them and having them pull their offer?"

I would advise you to put yourself in the hiring authority's shoes and understand this situation from their perspective: They want you. Their offer is proof of that point. They're not offering you this much because they are afraid you'll ask for more. They are making their rich offer because people in this position make this much, and because they think you're worth it and want you on board.

Now they've just gone through five of the best potential candidates for this position. Do you really think they want to walk away from you so they can call number two, the one they just passed over, to see if he is still interested after a week has passed? And will this person say yes? Probably not, if he is currently employed. And if he isn't employed, then is desperate ever as desirable as worthy?

You don't want to blow it when you are so close, and neither do they. They are concerned about possibly losing you. They don't know if you are interviewing with another company and are waiting for this competitor to make a better offer. That week waiting period will be a little unnerving to them, which is a good thing. It increases your negotiating leverage.

THE WARNING

Many years ago a recruiter solemnly told me the following, and I've never forgotten it. She said, "The person who interviewed before you was offered this job. But he asked for an increase in salary and they pulled the offer. You can do whatever you want to do, but if you want this job, then I suggest you accept what they are offering."

I quickly placed her tip into my "Bizarre, Insane Advice" file and prepared to negotiate for not just a little more money, but for a lot more—25% more on the base salary, a signing bonus, and another week of vacation.

The end result was this: I got everything I asked for. So long as your negotiating style is right, asking for a better package is almost never wrong.

ASKING FOR MORE

How high can you go? That depends on the salary range of your position. So, let's say you were offered a salary of $150,000, and the range is typically $140,000 to $180,000. Since your experience is not yet as extensive as that of people making the upper end of that range you might conclude, "I'd like to make $165,000."

The question now becomes, "What do I counter?"

For most people this questions sounds obvious. You counter with $165,000, right?

Wrong. In negotiating you ask for double the amount that you actually want. If you want $15,000 more you ask for $30,000. Your counter would be a request for a salary of $180,000. This is so that you have room to walk back your counteroffer until you meet in the middle. If the hiring authority counters $160,000, moving $10,000 closer to you, then you would either accept their offer or, if you're your nerves were still strong, you would counter by moving $10,000 closer to them: $170,000. This is the bracketing principle of negotiation. The acceptable midpoint is now crystal clear to all parties.

Negotiation needs to take your personal psychology into account. If asking for $180,000, or any sum significantly larger than the initial offer, keeps you from sleeping at night, then don't ask for it. Your quavering voice will let the hiring authority know that they do not need to meet your counter. Even your emailed responses will probably shout, "Stress response! Cortisol overload!"

If this is the case, then ask for what you are comfortable with. But please do not undervalue the impression you have made.

Besides, they just might accept your request for a $30,000 raise. It could be that their range is higher than your research estimated and because they want you, boom! You got it.

The counteroffer shouldn't stop at an additional salary request. Ask for an additional week or two of vacation. And ask for a $15,000 signing bonus. These signing bonuses are one of the easiest things to get, because CFOs understand how this is a one-time, non-recurring charge. They are so used to dealing with bigger issues, that these small, non-recurring expenses are almost never nixed, but they are rarely offered up front, so ask for it.

The big concern most people have is this: What if the size of my request angers them? What if it leads to a contentious negotiation that gets me started off on the wrong foot?

This is where you use mindsets to your advantage to keep this from happening.

THE WIN-WIN NEGOTIATOR

I like to make counteroffers by email. It gives them something in writing to analyze. It's more dispassionate. Sometimes what you say over the phone to create the mindset that you are a fair and flexible negotiator is overshadowed by the emotional impact of your request for much more money. And since what you said isn't in writing for them to review, your mindset may never get set, so to speak.

An email also keeps the hiring authority from being placed in the uncomfortable position of having to respond while trying to get over the shock of your counteroffer. With an email, he can review your offer, calm down, re-read the message, and then respond.

The mindset I want to create is of a fair, flexible negotiator who believes the final offer can be a win-win. And just like the other mindsets I've created, this one is the truth.

You can begin your email with the following.

> I am very excited to receive your offer. You will find my counteroffer below. But since we have never negotiated with each other I would like to introduce you to my approach. I aim for a win-win solution in every negotiation. I am always open to discussing and modifying my counteroffer(s) because I know we can find a creative, mutually agreeable solution.

The purpose of this intro is to remove fear, but I've heard some career coaches say, "This is unnecessary. They know that." To this I reply, "How could they know this if we've never negotiated before? Since some people are unreasonable negotiators, then why not address this fear up front?"

I want them to know that I am not the type to draw a line in the sand. If the counteroffer has to be modified in their favor, then I'm open to that.

What comes next is the style of the counteroffer, not the substance.

The email continues:

> I am countering your offer of a $150,000 with a request for $180,000. I will be happy to discuss, at length, how I think we can make this work for both of us. There are many creative options available that I'm confident would satisfy us both.
>
> Instead of two weeks of vacation I am requesting four. I had three weeks of vacation in my past two positions and believe that four will help me maintain my hardworking productivity throughout the year, year after year.
>
> Finally, I am requesting a $15,000 signing bonus.
>
> I look forward to discussing this counteroffer with you and making it work for both of us.

It is likely you will only get one week of extra vacation, but you may get two. That would be a nice "problem" to have, wouldn't it? And they may come back with a salary increase that takes you immediately to $165,000. If that happens, you could counter with $175,000, but I think that would be a mistake. After all, they've made a strong counteroffer that takes you to where they probably believe you want to be. They aren't playing games. I interpret this action to mean they want to end the negotiation by letting you achieve your negotiating goals. So trying to squeeze more money out of this negotiation would have a poor risk-reward relationship. It may result in you getting a small bump in additional salary at the cost of bad feelings.

UNEXPECTED GYRATIONS

What if you've made your counteroffer and they call you up to discuss your email. The first words out of the hiring authority's mouth are, "Your counter is a lot more than we have budgeted for this position. It's a deal breaker. It's too high."

The worst thing you could do is argue that it isn't too high, because this would turn the negotiation into a confrontation. Instead, follow the feel-felt-flexible-find formula. Its purpose is to neutralize negative emotions and reinforce the mindset that you are the ultimate win-win negotiator.

You can respond as follows:

> I understand how you *feel*. Many hiring authorities have *felt* the exact same way. But first I want you to know that I am a *flexible*, reasonable person, and nothing in this counteroffer is set in stone. And once we look at my counter in a different light, I think you'll *find* it's a win-win. Since this position doesn't have the budget for it, perhaps we can change the position slightly by giving it additional responsibilities. I could handle the following extra duties: X, X, and X. And that should more than justify my counteroffer.

I don't think most hiring companies would come back that strongly against your counteroffer, but if they do, and you make such a nonthreatening, firm and intelligent response, then this negotiation should add to your already strong reputation.

But what if the hiring authority comes back and says, "I'm sorry I have to tell you that we cannot change the position, and we do not have the money budgeted for this position to meet your additional salary request."

What do I say then?

I would say, "I understand. So can you meet me half way and bump the salary up to $165,000. Will that be within the budget?"

It could be the person you are dealing with is unfamiliar with negotiating and you need to help him reach the right conclusions. And if that is still more than is budgeted for this position, then I'd ask, "What is the amount you've budgeted?"

If they tell you a number that is $10,000 over the offer, then ask them, "Is your counteroffer now $160,000?" You ask this question because you can't assume things when it comes to money discussions. We need to hear it from his lips and then see it in writing.

If he says, "Yes it is. You drive a hard bargain." And if the other negotiating items were resolved, you could reply, "I gladly accept your offer and now these negotiating skills will be put to use for you." Then ask for an emailed and fed-exed copy of the adjusted offer letter.

But let me make this clear: I'm just responding to hypothetical questions. Initial offers typically have negotiating room.

One last question, "What if they had $10,000 worth of room left and refused to offer it?"

That would be a major red flag. When a company is completely inflexible about negotiating a pay increase to a new employee who they are trying to woo, then imagine how slim your chances are of receiving a raise once you get on board. So be careful about joining a company that is inflexible during the negotiation phase. Let this understanding guide you: If they treat you poorly on the front end, you will be treated much worse after arriving.

There are exceptions to this. A retained recruiter may have marketed himself to the hiring company as being able to make the negotiation process smooth and seamless. One of these guys once asked me, "If the company were to make the following offer would it be acceptable?"

If I said, "Yes," then how would I be able to come back and ask for more? It was a clever ploy, but since I wasn't born yesterday I replied, "I have no doubt whatsoever that we will be able to come to a mutually satisfactory agreement." Then, once the formal offer was made, I upset his apple cart with a higher salary request and more. He didn't like this, but he wasn't the one who was going to be paid for my years of hard work.

CASE STUDY: EMOTIONS MUST BE CONTROLLED

Negotiation involves money, ending the pain and suffering of unemployment, regaining that pep in one's step and, therefore, the time of negotiation is intensely emotional. Unfortunately, these emotions tend to sabotage those who negotiate for themselves. These emotions are so strong, they can even unhinge my clients while I am working with them.

One of my clients, an accomplished man with a post-graduate degree, was not a very confident person when it came to speaking or writing. I will call him Edward. Edward was competing for an internal promotion, and he was not the favored candidate. His boss, a man who lived in another state, would be interviewing him and another person within their company. Edward's competitor had enjoyed a close relationship with the hiring authority for many years and he had not.

His chances seemed slim, but as I told him, you will need to interview in such a strong way that your boss's boss—who would also be part of the interviewing process—supports your candidacy 100%. This will make your boss's decision very difficult.

He was supposed to receive a forty-five minute phone interview, but while he was hitting homerun after homerun during this interview, and receiving very positive feedback from his boss's boss, his boss said, "Okay Edward, sorry we have to end the interview early, but we do, and I want to thank you for your time. We'll announce who will be promoted this Friday." Click, sayonara, no you can't ask any questions, see ya!

Friday came and went and there was no news. Another Friday came and went and there was no news. Then early in the following week he found out he got the job! As he said to me, "Your system works."

The offer was not insignificant, but it was not what he felt that the job should pay. So, he wrote a counteroffer and sent it to me for my advice. His first draft left out the mindset forming language, and it also asked for a raise in an ineffective way. He wrote, "I believe that a greater than __ % increase [the increase he received] is justified...." And he offered a few reasons why he should get one.

His nerves were getting the better of him. This amounts to a counteroffer without a counter. He did not specify how much he was requesting. He merely stated that he believed he should get a better offer. His gentleness might be taken as timidity, and when the other side senses this your negotiating leverage vanishes.

I added language that helped shape the mindset that he was a fair and flexible negotiator who always seeks a win-win and also added a specific number. The response he got back was telling.

The internal HR person resent the initial offer letter. They were acting like his counteroffer did not exist and were refusing to budge. I was surprised their letter didn't contain a postscript saying, "This is all you're getting, bub."

This is one of the reasons why some "Human Resources" departments are often called "Resources" departments. There is often very little "human" involved in those shops that are poorly run. The least he could have done in the response to the counter was say, "Unfortunately, we have no room for increasing the salary," or, "This is the maximum salary we are allowed to offer." But instead, a kick in the teeth was all he offered Edward.

What should he do? Edward was mad. He felt he was being treated poorly—he was—and it angered him. So, he wanted to fire back his counteroffer buttressed by several arguments that stated why he was the best candidate, the one who brings the most value, and so on.

When we are angry we can make mistakes. HR would never resend an unmodified, initial offer letter without his boss's prompting. The message his boss was sending was clear: "There is no room for negotiation."

I said:

> Edward, your boss is telling you clearly that there will be no negotiating. Therefore, since he is the most important person in your career, the one who can promote you—as he just did—or fire you, who can increase your pay, or hold it steady, then you need to do whatever you can to become his trusted ally. Write him back a letter that says you enthusiastically accept this offer and will do all in your power to make him look good, and appear very smart for choosing you.

The last thing we wanted was his offer being pulled and given to the "more flexible" friend of his boss. He was the person his boss probably thought would get the job until Edward's stunning performance changed everything.

Not every negotiation is guaranteed success. Some offers are set in stone for a variety of reasons that can be both institutional and personal. The one thing we never want a negotiation session to achieve is wrenching defeat out of the jaws of victory.

EMOTIONAL CONTROL: JUMPING THE GUN

Fear can inspire us to fight, like Edward, or to fly, like June. She is an example of a client who was unable to control her emotions.

June had just secured a job offer that she really wanted, but they came in low on the initial salary offer. Someone with her experience, in her position, should receive about twenty percent more. I said, "Tell them you need five days to think about it and then send in your request for a thirty percent bump in salary along with the information that this was the industry-wide salary for someone with your expertise based on numerous conversations with recruiters, etc."

She said she did not want to wait five days before responding. She wanted to get started by the first of the month so she was going to reply to them that same day with her counter. She did, and they shot back a counter offer that only moved five percent toward where she wanted them to be.

Why the stingy counter? Her eagerness all but told them that she was dying to get this job and she lost all of her negotiating leverage. It is another example of the power of non-verbal communication. Responding too quickly says a lot. And here is the amazing thing: She thought she was about to get another offer from another company in the next two days. Had she asked for the five days, and gotten a second offer, her leverage would have increased exponentially. But she could not control her emotions and it hurt her ability to negotiate.

DO I ALWAYS COUNTER?

Yes, you always make a counteroffer and never immediately accept an offer. Immediate acceptance can trigger an unwanted response. For example, if you've ever thrown someone a low-ball offer on a used car, and the seller immediately accepted your offer, then are you jumping up and down for joy over your good fortune?

I doubt it. The chances are two thoughts are troubling you.

>Thought one: Heck! I know I could have done better.

>Thought two: Something must be wrong with this car.

Therefore, we should never immediately accept the first offer a hiring company makes. They may wonder if we are as good as they thought we were, because it appears we value ourselves less highly than they do.

Sometimes this hair-trigger response is due to a jobseeker's collision with his mindset. He formed a picture in his head of what they might offer him, and then their actual offer was much higher. He is overwhelmed by their offer. He thinks, "How can I ask for more? They'll think I am greedy. Heck, I'll think I'm greedy."

These mindsets affect all sorts of negotiations, but we need to destroy them and replace our self-perception with this reality:

> You ran in the right direction and appeared to be heads and tails better than your competition who kept running in the wrong direction. You came across as not only more competent, but also as more likable. They *want* someone like you on their team. So please stop being surprised by the strength of their offer.

THE GIFTS OF THE PATH

We have now arrived at the end of the path to job search success. We've covered a lot of ground and you've had to put in an amazing amount of effort. However, I feel certain that you've learned a few new skills and techniques that can help you for the rest of your life, and I hope you employ them.

Here is the testimony of eighteen-interview Jack, who recently wrote me a note to let me know how he is doing:

> Hi Tom,
>
> I have been meaning to send you a note to say Hi and let you know how my re-entry into engineering has gone. I have been at my company for just over a year and had my annual review last week. I received an OUTPERFORM and got one of the top rating of my office. A lot of what I had learned during our discussions I have applied to my everyday work with internal staff as well as with my clients.

I add this to give you another reason to be motivated to master this material. I know it will help you on your job search path, and will continue helping you after you land your dream job.

I tried to cover most of the important issues during the course of this book, but no book could cover everything. To cover this contingency I've developed a few principles to help guide you if your situation becomes cloudy and unclear.

22

The H.E.A.R.T. Principles

PRINCIPLES GUIDE OUR SEARCH

Even though I was starved and near delusional from a lack of sleep, I learned valuable lessons from the U.S. Army's Ranger School. One of the most important lessons was this: You can use different techniques, but you cannot violate the five principles of patrolling which are: Planning, reconnaissance, control, security and—my favorite, since my name is Tom Payne—common sense. These principles helped guide our actions when we were confronted by the unpredictable. And, if you were the patrol leader, and you were seen violating one of them, then you failed your patrol.

The principles of job search success are similar. Violate these principles and you will likely fail, particularly if you are competing against someone who follows them. And when you are confronted with a new situation, or a problem that this book fails to address, they will serve as guidelines to help you plot a new course.

The following list of five principles may leave out one or more that you believe to be important, but my purpose is not to create a comprehensive and exhausting list. Instead, it is an attempt to present, as simply as possible, a few of the more important, recurring themes that appeared throughout this book.

1. Human Nature.
2. Efficiency/Effectiveness/Energy.
3. Attitude: Always Positive, Always!
4. Rehearse.
5. Team.

1. HUMAN NATURE

The path to job search success involves realigning our search so that it works with human nature and not against it. To do this, we need to understand human nature. For example, once we know that non-verbal behaviors communicate more powerfully than our words do, we will put forth the necessary effort to master this form of communication. The benefit is such that the cost—or required effort—is less of an obstacle for us to overcome.

We also see how important our humanness is to job search. Because we are human we can feel job loss in our bones. It can beat us down and make us feel like a primate who was just trounced by the alpha male of the shrewdness. It can lower our sense of self, leading us to assign ourselves to the lowest rung of the dominance hierarchy, the place of maximum stress. Job loss can generate an emotional state that betrays us. But it need not, for there are ways to regain control of our emotional state and we have covered several of them.

Just remember this: You can be really smart—most of my clients are—and be mentally disabled by stress. I was counseling one woman who had the brainy distinction of being Phi Beta Kappa, but her lack of success on the path of job search was stressing her out. When I told her how this stress could take away her higher mental functions she declared, "That's it! I've been telling my friends, 'I think I'm getting more stupid by the day!' "

I said, "You probably are, but the good news is that this is reversible." You now have six techniques that can lessen the impact of the stress response and allow you to function cognitively at a high level. And this chapter will end with a seventh technique.

Human nature operates in states of cognitive ease and cognitive strain. Understanding how to avoid cognitive strain, and produce cognitive ease, is another way we can work with human nature. Data-dumping is an interviewing style that leads to cognitive strain and is to be avoided at all costs. On the other hand, clarity and repetition produce cognitive ease and we should employ these causes to achieve this desired effect.

Finally, we have a misguidance system that is designed to protect how we feel about ourselves. Once we know about our psychological immune system, and the way it can steer us away from reality, we can regain control of the wheel. We can use our power of reason to assess what it is we are doing wrong, and then make course corrections.

In short, we need to understand ourselves, embrace all of the psychological aspects of our nature, and structure job search accordingly.

2. EFFICIENCY/EFFECTIVENESS/ENERGY

One of the biggest problems jobseekers face is working efficiently and effectively, and maintaining their energy level to get through all of the laborious tasks of job search. For example, networking prior to developing our branding statement is ineffective, because the following can then happen:

> I network my way in front of a powerful businessperson, who has an enormous number of contacts, but I am unable to articulate the value that I bring to organizations, like the one he heads. He keeps waiting to hear me tell him why he should be interested in speaking with me, but never does.

Will this person introduce me to his world of contacts? Probably not. I failed to make the right impression and he would not risk me wasting the time of his friends and colleagues. One of my biggest networking assets has just been wasted.

To be efficient we need a well-thought out plan, and here is a sketch of one possibility:

1. First, we must gain control of our emotional state. If we are radiating negativity and a lack of confidence we will get nowhere. This battle is fought on many levels. It can begin with us adjusting our attitudes. We need to climb out of any hole the trauma of job loss may have dug for us, or else our job search will be tainted by a half-hearted effort. This enables us to master our non-verbal communication. The high-power pose exercise, deep breathing, method acting's visualization of peak moments in your life, visualizing yourself successfully interviewing, and regular, physical exercise are practices that lead to producing a positive, confident, emotional state. We then communicate this feeling to others through our non-verbal behaviors.

2. We must master the verbal component of our communication strategy by understanding our strengths, and articulating them through a branding statement. It can then be used for networking, informational interviewing, and job interviewing. Write your branding statement down and then rewrite it, edit, edit, edit, rehearse, rehearse, rehearse....

3. Start the story development process. And, same as above, "Write, edit, edit, edit, rehearse, rehearse, rehearse...."

4. Develop and execute a networking/informational-interviewing plan. First, reach out to people you know. Then research those who you don't know—making them a warm call—and reach out to them as well.

5. Conduct a videotaped mock interview to get a sense for how much work you need to do between now and the real thing. These videos can be very motivating. When we see how poorly we are presenting ourselves we are motivated to change. Or, when we finally see how well we are doing we gain a confident edge.

6. Develop answers to the typical questions interviewers ask. And script your strengths in a way that fits the opportunity.

7. Develop answers to suicide questions, and never dwell on your liabilities. State them briefly and, when possible,

bracket them with strengths.

There are other steps that are covered in the principles that follow, but for now we remain focused on efficiency, effectiveness and energy.

Efficiency conserves energy. Effectiveness focuses energy on mastering and employing techniques that are sound and proven. In practice many people fail to follow this effectiveness principle. Stories, for example, are one of the most powerful interviewing tools, but jobseekers typically fail to invest the time and energy required to develop at least ten of them.

Networking is also effective, but many waste their time spending hours online on job websites that they've already visited dozens of times. I am not saying these sites are a complete waste of time. Certainly LinkedIn® is a valuable networking tool, but when we focus primarily on websites instead of networking with human beings we are using our time inefficiently and ineffectively. Our words on a screen can never have the personal impact that a trained, influential voice can have.

Energy. You will need to tap into energy stores you may not currently possess. Therefore, invest in activities that recharge your batteries. Exercise is one of the most effective ways of reenergizing oneself and reducing the toxic, debilitating effects of chronic stress.

3. ATTITUDE: ALWAYS POSITIVE, ALWAYS!

We need to have positive attitudes about ourselves, our job-search prospects, positive answers to interview questions, a positive demeanor…in short, we always need to be positive, always!

Positivity is what transforms "I am a problem seeking a solution" into its positive counterpart: "I am a solution seeking a hiring authority's problems."

It also helps guide us in the development of effective answers to questions asking for a negative response. Questions like, "What are your weaknesses?" Most people hate this question. Its negative focus makes it a dreaded, poorly handled part of the interview. But

I love this question, because it allows me to answer a difficult question in a way that differentiates me from my competitors.

An important attitude that jobseekers must adopt is one wherein excuses are not tolerated. The U.S. Army had a very effective way of making sure this attitude was in place. If you ever made an excuse you would be asked, "Lieutenant, what is the maximum effective range of an excuse?"

There was only one answer, "0.0 meters, sir!"

But what if you just inherited a platoon full of slackers who proudly parade their lack of motivation, and today was your first day on the job. Who is to blame for their poor morale? You are, because this platoon is now yours. So, instead of worrying about diverting blame by making excuses you focus on turning them into worthwhile soldiers. Your energy is now focused on being the solution, and turning this problem into a solution.

Excuse making is a problem sustainer. It keeps the problem alive and well by diverting our attention away from solving it. When a person takes radical responsibility for their job search failures, they never make excuses just to feel better about a bad outcome. By holding themselves responsible for all outcomes, no matter what, a negative is turned into a positive. They ask, "What could I have done better?" They are solution-centered and they don't allow themselves the self-defeating luxury of not being accountable for their job search.

I was once posed this hypothetical question: "What if I was just brought in to fill an interviewing quota. What if Human Resources forced the hiring authority to interview at least three people, but the hiring authority knew beforehand he was going to hire his friend? Is my interviewing failure my fault even when the decision is foreordained."

My answer was a surprise, "Of course it is. Un-foreordain this decision. Show this person and *everyone else you interview with* why you are a far better choice." This approach was the one I made sure Edward applied—in the chapter on negotiating—and he un-foreordained the outcome that appeared to be set against him.

ALWAYS POSITIVE: THE FIXED CONTEST

We need to enter every competition as if we can prevail, even when everything seems to be fixed against us. Few outcomes were more foreordained than a Russian winning the 1958, height-of-the-Cold-War, Moscow-based, First International Tchaikovsky Competition.

Then a young Texan performed Rachmaninoff's Third Piano Concerto and received a standing ovation that lasted eight minutes.

The officials knew Van Cliburn had won, but they also knew they lived in a state with a very large Gulag. So they asked the Soviet leader, Nikita Khrushchev, if it was okay to award him the prize. Khrushchev asked if he had won. They said he had. Khrushchev probably shocked them with his response, "Give him the prize." What was thought to be foreordained was not.

How well would Van Cliburn have played if he approached this competition as if it was foreordained against him? With an attitude like that he would have been better served to just stay at home, but he embraced the challenge and won.

TURN EVERY NEGATIVE INTO A POSITIVE

Before I worked with them, some of my clients were ticking time bombs. They entered an interview dreading a specific question being asked that always caused them to stumble. During the interview, the pressure kept building. They worried, "He's going to ask the question. I just know it!" The stress levels were at high tide and the brain's centers governing complex thinking went black. Finally, when the interviewer asked the dreaded question, a stress-hormone-addled simpleton responded with an incoherent, unconvincing answer. The interview was over. The hiring authorities literally felt the interviewee's pain and it made them recoil.

I met a talented woman while she was preparing for an interview and she told me interviewers would look at her resume and say, "You were on such a nice trajectory in the early part of your career. But then, right here," they would point at a spot on her resume that she knew all-too-well, and continue, "things changed. What happened?"

She said this was where the interview always went downhill. She had no good answer for this question that she dreaded. It made her visibly uncomfortable. She asked me, "What can I do?"

So I asked her, "Okay, what happened?"

She told me how her life went through a perfect storm that year. A serious, promising relationship ended, a parent died, and there were a few other personal upsets. She was heartbroken, sad, and depressed. She was simply human.

She said, "I just needed to take some time off to pull myself together. And so I left the corporate world, did some consulting and now I am ready to get back into the corporate fray. But this issue comes up every interview and I don't know what to do about it."

She was hypnotized by the negative and could not see negativity's flipside, the positive. So, I told her to hope they asked this question during her next interview so she could say:

> Nobody wants to go through really dark and difficult times, but we all experience them. The important thing is not how far you get knocked down, but how you respond to the experience. During the time you are asking about I went through a period of personal upheaval that required me to take some time off. So I did. I then worked in a consulting capacity to get back on my feet and learn new skills. This trial did what most trials do. It made me stronger. And now I am ready to reenter the corporate arena and utilize the new skills I've gained.

She interviewed shortly thereafter and was hired. Her answer likely inspired feelings of admiration. The former black spot on her resume became a memorable story of overcoming adversity.

Every weakness has a strength and every negative has a positive side. Our focus needs to be on the light and not the darkness. Always be positive. Always! And no excuses. Ever.

4. REHEARSAL

This is a principle that could also be called "mastery." Without following this principle Jack would never have been as confident and relaxed as he was through eighteen interviews.

We begin by creating great material, but our job is incomplete until we master it. Mastery is the foundation of confidence. I looked forward to interviews because I knew I had powerful answers to virtually any question they might ask. It enabled me to deliver my winning message with passion, poise and conviction. But this required work, lots of work. It required many rounds of editing and rehearsal before I was able to deliver my material effectively.

I've given hundreds of thoroughly scripted and rehearsed presentations. At the end of training classes and seminars I pass out anonymous evaluations. Or seminar attendees are sent a SurveyMonkey survey by email. And as of this writing I've never heard, "Tom, you sound scripted. You don't sound natural." Typically I get a five-out-of-five rating and people comment upon how passionately I deliver the message.

If you sound too rehearsed there is only one solution: Rehearse more. This is counter-intuitive, but it works the following way. I rehearse until the material is mine. I know it and own it. It is a part of my thought process, and when I express these thoughts it is as natural as breathing.

We edit our material—stories, value statements, etc.—to make them less wordy and more efficient. We rehearse to make our presentation more effective.

Have you ever watched one of the many TED Talks that are available online? They all have this characteristic: Flawless delivery. This confident presentation of their ideas is part of the reason why they are so influential and popular.

Guess what? Some TED Talks are rehearsed over 100 times before they are recorded and shared on their platform. "Dr. Jill Bolte-Taylor rehearsed her TED talk 200 times. It's been viewed 15 million times and Oprah invited her to be a guest on her show. Dr.

Jill's TED talk transformed her career."[1] The more she rehearsed, the less rehearsed she seemed.

Rehearsal is also a principle of military training. Why do soldiers play endless, expensive war games, rehearsing for a real combat situation? Because in a threatening, chaotic environment a soldier will perform as he has trained. Since the job interview can seem both threatening and confusing, rehearsing is a sound principle to follow. For when an interviewer interrupts you, or tries to trip you up, you will continue to perform as you have trained.

5. TEAM

You can successfully go through this job search process alone, but you will be putting yourself at a major disadvantage. There are simply too many benefits to be gained by working with others.

Your team should include an accountability group. If you can connect with other jobseekers and participate in an accountability group, then by all means do so.

I especially want to encourage men to take this step. As Deborah Tannen famously noted, men don't like to ask for directions. This observation went viral and became a truism overnight. But what did not receive much attention was the reason she gave for men not asking for directions.

According to Tannen, men are driven by status, their place in the hierarchy, and asking for directions moves a man down the status ladder. Or, as she put it:

> When you offer information, the information itself is the message. But the fact that you have the information, and the person you are speaking to doesn't, also sends a metamessage of superiority.[2] If relations are inherently

---

[1] The online link to the article this quotation comes from is: http://www.forbes.com/sites/carminegallo/2014/03/17/the-one-habit-that-brilliant-ted-speakers-practice-up-to-200-times/

[2] Communication always involves a relationship between the participants in face-to-face talk. Because of the activity of the cognitive unconscious, it is about, "How am I being treated?" Metamessages are secondary

> hierarchical, then the one who has more information is framed as higher up on the ladder by virtue of being more knowledgeable and competent. From this perspective, finding one's own way is an essential part of the independence that men perceive to be the prerequisite for self-respect. If self-respect is bought at the cost of a few extra minutes in travel time, it is well worth the price.[3]

To ask for directions puts men one-down, and makes the person who knows the directions one-up. Men tend to be hampered by the sense that reaching out for help puts them one-down, and turning to someone for help puts their independence at risk. Then, as their psychological immune system kicks in to protect their self-respect, they choose to go it alone. Men tend to avoid asking for help and try to find their own way down job-search's path.

Most women don't suffer from this same issue and they readily turn to others for help. This is a strength, not a weakness. So, gentlemen, recognize that your instincts move you in this direction. You may not aspire to be the alpha-male of the shrewdness, but you are unlikely to willingly put yourself one-down on the ladder of status. Now that you know this tendency exists, resist it. Teams are powerful ways of expediting the search process, staying positive through the encouragement of others, and getting new ideas.

An accountability group will help you follow your plan and do things you don't think are possible now. For example, let's say you are introverted and find the idea of networking too nerve-wracking to attempt. Simply seeing others talking about how they did it—other people who aren't any better than you—helps give you the confidence to do it also. You think, "If that person can do it, then so can I." Many organizations that try to build healthy habits—for example, Weight Watchers—use the power of groups to help people achieve goals they failed to achieve on their own.

---

messages that can communicate the nature of our relationship. The words say one thing, but the intent of the message may say another.
[3] Deborah Tannen, *You Just Don't Understand: Women and Men in Conversation* (New York: HarperCollins Publishers, 1990), p. 62

TEAM AND COGNITIVE DIVERSITY

Different people with different backgrounds have different experiences that shape the way they think, and this gives them unique perspectives. There was a time when most people in the American business world were white men. There were differences in their background and experiences, but nothing as different as the unique perspectives offered by women, or blacks and Latinos.

People who are virtually the same will tend to think alike. Our experiences have conditioned us to do so. What is helpful is for people who are cognitively diverse to get together to discuss problems that need solving. The members of a cognitively diverse team think differently, and their different approaches enable out-of-the-box thinking.

Cognitive diversity is a powerful way corporations are tackling some of their most difficult challenges. An example of this is a company named Innocentive. Businesses post a problem on their website and invite their community of over 100,000 problem solvers to view the problem. The problem solvers then decide whether the reward for solving the problem is adequate or not. If it is, and the problem is suited to their skillsets, then they can attempt to solve it.

Innocentive solves 40% of the problems they accept. This is a remarkable achievement, because these are the toughest problems, ones that a corporation determined was beyond their ability. By tapping into this rich pool of cognitively diverse thinkers they are able to achieve solutions faster.

The power of cognitive diversity can be used by jobseekers by being a part of a team. Since everyone tends to think inside the box of their own, established way of thinking, it is a great benefit to discuss your job search questions with others to get their "out-of-your-box" thinking.

TEAM: A JOB-SEARCH COACH

Your personal team should include a job search coach if one is available at a price you can afford. Coaches aren't necessary for job search success, but they do accelerate the growth and development process. Even the world's best golfers, baseball players, and business executives utilize coaches.

The Career Transitions Center of Chicago (CTC) offers one of the most reasonable deals I've ever seen, with access to over thirty highly-skilled coaches.[4] If you have a good local program in your city, then by all means research the program. If it offers valuable training, then take advantage of it. Large churches and synagogues, your Chamber of Commerce, alumni associations, often offer excellent programs, or know of them.

If there are no local options, then the CTC offers virtual programs for those who are not in the Chicago area. I do not volunteer for the virtual sessions, but the CTC has excellent coaches available.

I also work as a coach for private clients. My programs are customized and I am driven by a desire to make my clients succeed. If you are interested in exploring the use of my services, then check out my website, tompayne.com, and contact me.

I will now close with the story of a client I recently coached. It will provide you with the seventh technique to help you regain control of your emotional state. Her achievement inspires me and it fills me with joy.

SOMETIMES YOU NEED A COACH

A private client of mine, who I will call Tess, was like a soldier suffering from PTSD. She had been out of work for nineteen months and had failed in fifty-nine, straight job interviews. She was very smart (MBA from the University of Chicago), accomplished, likable, and engaging, but she no longer believed in herself. A tape kept playing in her head that said, "Loser! What happened to you? Your career looked so promising. Why did you screw it up?"

---

[4] Twelve weeks of coaching, one session per week, with a variety of professional coaches to choose from, and many other services, for $300. But if you are a member of a sponsoring institution—DePaul University, Loyola University, etc.—then the cost is $200.

Nineteen months of negative self-talk can make you a stranger to yourself. She no longer knew who she was and she desperately needed to reconnect with her real self before she disappeared. So, we had a conversation:

Me: Are you smart?

Tess: Yes. I believe so.

Me: What makes you think that?

She looked at me a little surprised. My tone was challenging. I was saying, "Prove it." She then said:

Tess: Well, I went to a distinguished undergrad program and did very well. I also got an MBA from one the top programs in the country.

Me: Oh, so you have objective evidence that you are smart. This is a fact, not a fantasy, am I right?

Tess: Yes.

Me: Are you likable?

And so the conversation went. It became something of a game, and she would smile with each question. I finally ended it by saying, "When I tell you that you have every reason to be confident, because you are smart, accomplished, likable, and engaging, I am not saying things that aren't true to try and make you feel better. I'm sharing objectively verifiable facts. So will you please start believing me, and believe in yourself."

After our conversation she told me she would wake up each morning and say, "I'm smart and I have objective evidence to prove it. I am likable and engaging for the following reasons...."

Her negative self-talk was now replaced by positive self-talk based on reality. A week later she interviewed with a company and was hired. Their salary offer was $20,000 more than her previous salary. This indicates she was able to transform their "need to fill a slot" into "an intense desire to have her fill this slot."

Positive self-talk is a powerful way of reconnecting with the real you, not the wounded you who may be anxious about the future. It is not about making affirmations that are rooted in unreality. It is about affirming strengths that are objectively verified by the results you have produced.

Yes, I helped her with her stories, her branding statement, rehearsing, and so on. But the most important thing I did was help her regain control of her emotional state. Until this happened she was destined to fail.

Could she have done this on her own? Possibly, but I doubt it. Sometimes you get thrown down a hole that is so deep you cannot climb out of it without having a helping hand. What she needed was someone who saw who she really was and radiated confidence in her until she could finally feel what her coach felt.

Human nature has this capability: we can feel what others feel. When the hiring authority feels our anxiety, fear and a lack of confidence this can outweigh the objective reality that each one of us may actually be a great hire. So, we need to regain our confidence, our enthusiasm and zest for life. Then, when the 60th job opportunity comes around, the same person who failed the previous 59 times can become the irresistible candidate who receives an unexpectedly rich offer.

When I spoke to Tess after she received her job offer, I could feel what she felt: pure joy and happiness. Her brutal slog through the wilderness was longer than she would have liked it to be, but this made leaving the wilderness one of the greatest days of her life.

AND NOW WE MUST PART

Dear Reader,

Thank you for taking this journey with me to the very end of the book. I suspended other projects to pour my heart and soul into this book, because I care deeply about those who are going through the job-search process. I hope this single-minded focus resulted in a work that will help you in the short- and long-term.

Ultimately the fate of all independent authors, like me, rests in the hands of their readers. If many of these readers took the time to write a review, even one that is one sentence long, then this work would be virtually guaranteed success. But without reviews this book is destined to be overlooked by those who might be helped the most by it.

Please ask yourself, "Did this book offer an original way of approaching the job search process? Did it teach me valuable skills that I did not possess before? Did I learn about the importance of non-verbal communication, and how to control these behaviors to communicate the right message? Did I learn about mindsets and how to use them in the interview, and in negotiating my best offer? Could this book help others who are struggling to win the all-important, internal battle that can spell the difference between job search success or defeat?"

I've personally witnessed my system help those who were on the verge of giving up, people like Tess. Your review can help my book reach these same people. Therefore, I am asking you to please take a moment, and write a review. Your honest, candid feedback would be appreciated.

In parting, I hope you have learned some valuable new lessons, and have already begun to apply them. The path to job search success involves hard work, but this investment of time and energy can equip you with new skills that enrich the rest of your life.

Finally, if you are in the midst of job search, then I pray this book has given you a real, enduring hope. This job-search system works, providing you put in the work. Just remember that whoever you are, wherever you are on life's path, you are a solution to some hiring authority's problems. So, with this positive attitude always at the forefront of your mind, march forward with confidence and your solution will find a home.

My best,

Tom Payne

Acknowledgements

I'd like to thank all of the people who appeared on my radio program "You're Hired." I found myself learning important new lessons as I interviewed them to record free, downloadable podcasts on important job search topics.

Laura Sterkel was my first guest and she spoke about the central importance of the value statement. At the time, she was the Program Director for the CTC and she was a great help to me and many others. Sharon Krohn was my second guest and she is a highly valued volunteer coach at the Career Transitions Center of Chicago (CTC).

Anita Jenke, the Executive Director for the CTC, helped jobseekers formulate a plan to give their job search structure and focus. Kerry Obrist, the CEO and owner of More Access Solutions, spoke about how difficult it is for the disabled to find work in the U.S., and yet how incredibly productive these workers are. Orla Castanien described the Peak Moments exercise to help jobseekers discover their strengths.

Professor Michael Milco, who has an active counseling practice, shared his insights on coping. He has done some fascinating research on African refugees and their need to cope both during their time in a refugee camp and the subsequent repatriation. This returning home can be the most difficult step of all.

Dr. Jane Kise, who is highly regarded throughout the MBTI® community, spoke about Type and its relationship to careers. Marty Gahbauer shared his deep informational interviewing expertise. Steven Steinfeld coached those over forty on how to find a job, TM Napa covered fearless networking, Howard Fox spoke about LinkedIn®, and Marcia McMahon offered tips about resumes. Thanks to all of you. These podcasts are free and downloadable at www.tompayne.com.

Others at the CTC have been extremely helpful. Emily Drake, the idea-rich program director, has been a delight to work with. Jim Boysen, another volunteer coach, is someone I like to team up with. He does a great job with videotaped mock interviews.

Those who have written excellent works that detail the recent insights of neuroscience and other brain-related fields were particularly helpful. Dr. John Ratey's book entitled *Spark* is one of the best books I've read on the powerful mind-body connection. Dr. Robert Sapolsky's book, *Why Zebras Don't Get Ulcers*, was entertaining and rich in scientific insights. Timothy D. Wilson's, *Strangers to Ourselves*, is a well-written, fascinating book and well worth reading. But the magnum opus of this field is *Thinking, Fast and Slow*, the work of the Nobel Prize winning author, Daniel Kahneman. As mentioned previously, it is a dense, slow read, but if you are interested in this field it is well worth the effort.

I'd like to thank Amy Cuddy for her research and her response to my inquiry. Clients of mine who have seen her TED Talk have told me it was inspiring. I highly recommend it and have seen it myself several times.

Finally, I'd like to thank my wife, Joni, for her editorial advice and encouragement.

Made in the USA
Charleston, SC
06 July 2015